D1472900

HOW TO LOCATE REVIEWS OF PLAYS AND FILMS

A Bibliography of Criticism
from the Beginnings to the Present

by

GORDON SAMPLES

The Scarecrow Press, Inc.
Metuchen, N.J.   1976

Library of Congress Cataloging in Publication Data

Samples, Gordon.
    How to locate reviews of plays and films.

    Includes index.
    1. Theater--Reviews--Bibliography. 2. Moving-
pictures--Reviews--Bibliography. I. Title.
Z5781.S19 [PN1707]   016.791   76-3509
ISBN 0-8108-0914-1

3-1303-00052-9447

Copyright © 1976 by Gordon Samples

Printed in the United States of America

For
KEITH & TROY,
both critics and performers
at an early age

CONTENTS

PREFACE

Literary criticism, and in particular, criticism of plays and films, is among the most frequent requests of research and reference specialists. It is for this reason that this guide has been compiled.

Within most sections the selected items are chronologically arranged by years covered, not by publication date of the books. Thus, by first determining the production or publication dates of the play or film in question, one may more easily spot criticism for that year or period of time. This method also throws together items by genre; e.g., the Medieval Stage, the Baroque Stage; or the silent film and the experimental film. By first using the groupings of the table of contents in conjunction with the chronologies and the index, one should be directed more quickly to the material desired.

In searching for material, it is important to distinguish between a review and a piece of serious criticism. The review announces a play or film, describes its subject, discusses its method and technical qualities, its players, its directors, and examines its merits as compared with other similar works. Its function is to give its reader an accurate idea of the play or film in order that he may decide whether he wishes to read the script or attend a performance. A critique is far more judicious than a review; the critic makes a critical examination of a work with a view to determining its nature and assessing its value according to some established standards. The critic usually writes about works which already have some standing and which are not brand new. Even so, the boundary line between the two forms is very uncertain, and the reader may be confused to find overlapping in some indexing services and collections of articles. Walter Kerr, for example, differentiates between reviewing and criticism by suggesting that the critic assumes his reader has seen the work under discussion, and the reviewer that he has not.

A section on play synopses has been included for those drama coaches looking for special scenes, monologues, and types of plays, as well as for those seeking to determine controlling agencies for performances. This section advises the reader as to cast and set requirements, subjects, fees, availability of non-published or manuscript-only type plays, etc. The basic controlling agencies are included here; however, many plays and musicals are controlled by the individual play publisher or the composer's agent. This information should appear on the back of the title page of the play. An example of a type of play for which it is very difficult to determine the controlling agency is the short play, or one-act play of which the publisher is not known, or which has never been published as a separate or in an anthology. In such cases a considerable amount of searching is necessary.

Regarding film criticism, one should also determine if contemporary reviews are sufficient for older films, or if a present-day, new perspective would be better. In the last few years movies and their audiences have become more sophisticated, resulting in a challenge to the critics to likewise reflect the cinema scene. Thus later reviews are often placed in a sociological, psychoanalytical, or other perspective. This is important to the researcher, as opinions of films change with the years. Some become dated and some which when first released were not so favorably praised emerge as classics; or just the opposite may prove to be true. By checking the annotation in the bibliography one may determine the vintage of the review.

The study of the film is increasing all over the world. In the United States alone there are now 96 separate institutions where one may major in film. Besides this, some 300 colleges offer one or more courses in film study. Eighteen years ago American universities offered a scant 600 film courses. Today, there are more than 2,500. Classic films, current films, foreign films, underground films and experimental films are all given critical consideration. There are more books about films being published and more international film festivals than ever before.

Unfortunately, most indexing services are slow. Some run a year or two behind. Even those which are issued monthly may take up to six months to enter reviews. As for foreign films, they may be released in the United States several years after first being shown in the country of their origin. Often, upon arriving, they have had title changes. Thus original release dates cannot be completely relied on, so several years following the release date should be checked.

One should be forewarned not to give up when many references prove fruitless in searching. No indexing service is complete, so additional searching under the direction of a reference specialist may be necessary to locate the world's ever-growing and astounding number of plays and films.

Gordon Samples

San Diego State University
California
June 1975

"Do you come to the play without knowing what it is?"

"O, yes, Sir, yes, very frequently; I have no time to read play-bills; One merely comes to meet one's friends, and shew that one's alive."

--from _Evelina_, Letter 20. Fanny Burney, 1778.

PLAYS

CHRONOLOGY OF STUDY GUIDES

12th c. B.C. -
17th c. A.D.

Nicoll, Allardyce. Masks, Mimes and Miracles:
Studies in the Popular Art. N.Y., Har-
court, 1931; N.Y., Cooper Sq., 1963.
Traces the history of mime in the theatre with
emphasis on the Commedia dell'arte; includes
roles, major actors, scenarii; covers earliest
times from the Greek region of the Dorians
through the 17th century.

9th c. B.C.

Mantzius, Karl. A History of Theatrical Art
in Ancient and Modern Times. N.Y.,
Peter Smith, 1937. 6 vols.
A comprehensive classical study. Vol. 1: The
Earliest Times. Dancing, disguises, and mum-
meries; Chinese, Japanese, Indian, Greek and
Roman theatres.

9th c. B.C. -
20th c.

Cheney, Sheldon. The Theatre: Three Thousand Years of Drama, Acting and Stage-
craft. Rev. ed. N.Y., Longmans, Green,
1952.
A comprehensive historical manual of the theater covering all aspects, periods, and countries.

8th c. B.C. -
20th c.

Arlington, Lewis Charles. Chinese Drama from
Earliest Times until Today. Shanghai,
1930; N.Y., B. Blom, 1966.
A panoramic study of the art in China, tracing
its origin and describing its actors, costumes
and make-up, superstitions and stage slang, ac-
companying music and musical instruments; includes synopses of 30 plays.

6th c. -
5th c. B.C.

Flickinger, Roy Caston. Greek Theatre and Its
Drama. 4th ed. Chicago, University of
Chicago Press, 1960.
An account of the origin, influences, customs,
festivals, and theatres.

5th c. B.C.

Beare, William. The Roman Stage; a Short
History of Latin Drama in the Time of the

Republic. 3rd ed. N.Y., Barnes & Noble,
1965.
An account of drama of Ancient Rome in its
historical setting, discussing the plays, the
stage, the spectators, the organization of the
theatres, etc.

5th c. B.C.   Gargi, Balwant. Theatre in India. N.Y.,
                       Theatre Arts Books, 1962.
                   Most complete and authoritative in any language,
                   covers history of Sanskrit drama, classical In-
                   dian dance and the modern stage, folk opera,
                   market-place puppet and shadow plays.

3rd c. B.C. -   Nagler, A. M. Sources of Theatrical History.
19th c.   N.Y., Theatre Annual, 1952.
                   An anthology of theatrical history from the
                   Greeks to the end of the 19th century, as edited
                   from contemporary accounts, archival material,
                   etc.

3rd c. B.C. -   Brandon, James R. Theatre in Southeast Asia.
20th c.   Cambridge, Harvard University Press, 1967.
                   Presents basic facts about the theatre as it ex-
                   ists and functions: historical background; the-
                   atre as art; theatre as an institution; theatre
                   as communication; includes major theatre genres
                   as performed in 1964.

3rd c. B.C. -   Nicoll, Allardyce. World Drama from Aeschy-
20th c.   lus to Anouilh. London, Harrap, 1949.
                   Vigorous survey tracing and evaluating the de-
                   velopment of the drama.

3rd c. B.C. -   Cole, Toby, and Helen K. Chinoy, ed. Actors
20th c.   on Acting: the Theoriés, Techniques, and
                       Practices of the Great Actors of All Times
                       as Told in Their Own Words. New rev.
                       ed. N.Y., Crown, 1970.
                   A collection of actors' views on acting from
                   Plato to Joseph Chaikin (1969); divided by coun-
                   try and period: Greece, Rome, Middle Ages,
                   Italy, Spain, England, France, Germany, Ire-
                   land, Soviet Union, and America. The material
                   is arranged chronologically with a general al-
                   phabetical index and a classified index by acting
                   fundamentals.

330-1453 A.D.   Byron, Robert. The Byzantine Achievement;
                       an Historical Perspective, A.D. 330-1453.
                       N.Y., Knopf, 1929.
                   Surveys the Byzantine Empire as to historical
                   image and anatomy: fusion, chronology, trade,
                   culture, etc.

500-1500

Chambers, Edmund K.   The Mediaeval Stage.
Oxford, Clarendon Press, 1903.   2 vols.
Contains material roughly covering the period
500-1500 A.D.: the minstrelsy, folk drama,
religious drama, etc.

500-1700

Shergold, N. D.   A History of the Spanish Stage
from Medieval Times until the End of the
Seventeenth Century.   Oxford, Clarendon
Press, 1967.
Gives a complete account of the way in which
plays were staged in Spain from the Middle
Ages until about 1700; covers early religious
and secular drama; the public playhouse, the
court theatre, and the morality plays; texts of
the plays are discussed and fully indexed.

500-1700

Mantzius, Karl.   A History of Theatrical Art
in Ancient and Modern Times.   N.Y.,
Peter Smith, 1937.   6 vols.
A comprehensive classical study.   Vol. 2:
Middle Ages and the Renaissance.   Ecclesias-
tical and secular plays, Italian Comedy.

789-1699

Hawkins, Frederick William.   Annals of the
French Stage from Its Origin to the Death
of Racine.   Grosse Pointe, Mich., Scholarly Press, 1968.
Covers the period of 789-1699 for history and
criticism.

849-1616

Tucker, Martin and others, ed.   The Critical
Temper; a Survey of Modern Criticism on
English and American Literature from the
Beginning to the 20th Century.   N.Y.,
Frederick Ungar, 1969.   3 vols.
Research compiled from scholarly and critical
journals of literary history and opinion, studies
of a writer, critical interest on a literature,
period or esthetic movement.   Vol. 1:   From
Old English to Shakespeare (849-1616).

975-1700

Harbage, Alfred.   Annals of the English Stage,
975-1700.   Rev. ed.   London, Methuen,
1964.
Analytical record of all plays, extant or lost,
chronologically arranged and indexed by author,
title, dramatic company, etc.   Foreign plays
translated or adapted are included.   Location
of plays is given if extant.

12th c. -19th c.

Martinovitch, Nicholas N.   The Turkish Theatre.   N.Y., Theatre Arts, 1933.

Surveys the popular theatre: Orta Oiunu;
Meddah; and Karagoz as to origins, staging,
and representative scenes and plays.

1300-1666   Wickham, Glynne. Early English Stages, 1300-
                     1666. London, Routledge & Kegan Paul,
                     1959-1962. 2 vols.
               Attempts to trace the history of English stage-
               craft from its beginnings to the Restoration of
               the Monarchy; contains detailed notes and
               sources.

late 14th c.   Keene, Donald. Nō; the Classical Theatre of
                     Japan. Tokyo, Kodansha International,
                     1966.
               A pictorial history of the Nō, giving background
               of performances, music and dances, the staging,
               roles and their costumes.

1466-1966   Jones, Willis Knapp. Behind Spanish American
                     Footlights. Austin, University of Texas
                     Press, 1966.
               Covers nearly five centuries of the Latin
               American theatrical scene.

1486-1965   Gassner, John. Directions in Modern Theatre
                     and Drama. N.Y., Holt, Rinehart & Win-
                     ston, 1966.
               An expanded edition of the author's Form and
               Idea in Modern Theatre. Besides being a valu-
               able critical overview of the theatre, the book
               contains a chronology of modern theatre giving
               a bird's-eye view of important developments in
               the theatre from 1486 to 1965. Critical articles
               by other writers such as Bertram Joseph,
               Strindberg, Henry Adler, Edward Albee, Mar-
               vin Rosenberg are included. Titles of plays
               criticized appear in the index.

1497-1642   Holzknecht, K. J. Outlines of Tudor and
                     Stuart Plays, 1497-1642. London, Methuen,
                     1963.
               Critical comments, biographical information;
               describes each major figure.

1497-1642   Ribner, Irving, comp. Tudor and Stuart Drama.
                     N.Y., Appleton-Century-Crofts, 1966.
               Bibliography giving ample coverage of scholar-
               ship in the field published since 1920.

1500-1720   Clark, William Smith. The Early Irish Stage;
                     the Beginnings to 1720. Oxford, Clarendon
                     Press, 1955.

An account of theatricals in Ireland beginning
with the old Moralities and Mystery plays,
late Middle Ages to 1720.

1530-1800   Baur-Heinhold, Margarete. The Baroque
         Theatre; a Cultural History of the 17th and
         18th Centuries. N.Y., McGraw-Hill, 1967.
Includes the courts, the public, the players,
the plays, the stages and the theatres, with
chronological tables for Spain, England, France,
Italy, Germany, Netherlands, Denmark, Russia,
1530-1800. Illustrated with photographs, paint-
ings and drawings.

1558-1603   Chambers, Edmund K. The Elizabethan Stage.
         Oxford, Clarendon Press, 1923. 4 vols.
Encompasses the dramatic activity during the
reign of Queen Elizabeth (1558-1603). Contains
the court, control of the stage, the companies,
the playhouses, plays and playwrights.

1593-1616   Mantzius, Karl. A History of Theatrical Art
         in Ancient and Modern Times. N.Y.,
         Peter Smith, 1937. 6 vols.
A comprehensive classical study. Vol. 3:
Shakespeare Period in England.

1600-1699   Bentley, Gerald Eades, ed. The 17th Century
         Stage. Chicago, University of Chicago
         Press, 1968.
A collection of critical essays by contemporaries
of the period.

1600-1699   Mantzius, Karl. A History of Theatrical Art
         in Ancient and Modern Times. N.Y.,
         Peter Smith, 1937. 6 vols.
A comprehensive classical study. Vol. 4:
Molière and the Theatre in France of the 17th
Century.

1600-1799   Lough, John. Paris Theatre Audiences in the
         17th and 18th Centuries. London, Oxford
         Univ. Press, 1957.
A study of the spectators for whom Corneille,
Molière, Racine, Voltaire, Marivaux and Beau-
marchais wrote, and the influence exercised on
their plays by the audiences of the time; based
on contemporary documents.

1600-1899   Varneke, B. V. History of the Russian Thea-
         tre; Seventeenth through Nineteenth Century.
         N.Y., Macmillan, 1951.
Traces the history of Russian theatre from the

folk roots through the 19th century; gives information on plays, playwrights; excerpts from
contemporary criticism.

1600-1917   Slonium, Mark L'vovich. Russian Theatre
                        from the Empire to the Soviets. Cleve-
                        land, World Pub. Co. , 1961.
                   Dramatic history and criticism covering plays,
                   operas, playwrights, and theatre crafts.

1603-1642   Bentley, Gerald Eades. The Jacobean and
                        Caroline Stage. Oxford, Clarendon Press,
                        1941-1968.   7 vols.
                   Details dramatic companies and players, plays
                   and playwrights, theatrical customs for the
                   Jacobean Stage during the reign of James I
                   (1603-1625) and the Caroline Stage during the
                   reign of Charles I (1625-1642).

1603-20th c.   Ernst, Earle. The Kabuki Theatre. N. Y. ,
                        Oxford University Press, 1956.
                   Discusses the background, physical theatre and
                   its evolution, the audience and its attitudes, the
                   elements of a performance, the stage, the ac-
                   tors and their characters, since the appearance
                   of Kabuki at the end of the 16th century.

1603-20th c.   Gunji, Masakatsu. Kabuki. Tokyo, Kodansha
                        International, 1969.
                   A pictorial history discusses the spirit of Ka-
                   buki, the actors, plays and playwrights, thea-
                   tre and stage machinery, audience and per-
                   formances.

1637-1974   O'Haodha, Michael. Theatre in Ireland.
                        Totowa, N. J. , Rowman and Littlefield,
                        1974.
                   Traces the development of the Irish theatre
                   since the building of the first theatre in Dublin
                   in 1637 through the founders of the National
                   Theatre, Synge, Abbey Theatres, O'Casey,
                   Lady Gregory, Yeats, MacLiammoir, etc. , to
                   the current theatrical hopefuls.

1645-1930   Fülöp-Miller, René, and Joseph Gregor. The
                        Russian Theatre; Its Character and History
                        with Especial Reference to the Revolution-
                        ary Period. N. Y. , B. Blom, 1930.
                   A pictorial study covers the theatre of the
                   Tsars, theatre of the Nobles, theatre of the
                   Bourgeoise, and the People's theatre, with in-
                   formation on the "curve of development," the
                   Russian actor, the Ballet, etc.

1660-1700   Summers, Montague. The Restoration Theatre.
                        N. Y. , Macmillan, 1934.
                    An authoritative history covering the plays,
                    players, theatres, the audience, and the cus-
                    toms of pit, box, and gallery as told through
                    citations, allowing the Restoration theatre to
                    tell its own story.

1660-1800   The London Stage, 1660-1800; a Calendar of
                        Plays, Entertainments and Afterpieces, To-
                        gether with Casts, Box-receipts and Con-
                        temporary Comment. Carbondale, Southern
                        Illinois University Press, 1960-1968.   5
                        vols. in 11 pts.
                    Contemporary comments compiled from play-
                    bills, newspapers, box-office receipts, theatri-
                    cal diaries of the period. Its arrangement is
                    by theatre season and by day. Each entry
                    gives the play presented that day by each Lon-
                    don theatre, with cast, comment on the per-
                    formance.

1660-1800   The London Stage; a Critical Introduction, by
                        Emmett L. Avery and others. Carbondale,
                        Southern Illinois University Press, 1968.
                        5 vols.
                    Contains the critical introductions to each of
                    the five volumes as listed in The London Stage,
                    1660-1800.

1660-1830   Genest, John, ed. Some Account of the English
                        Stage from the Restoration in 1660 to 1830.
                        Bath, H. E. Carrington, 1832.   10 vols.
                    Covers plays, players and playwrights of the
                    period, including contemporary criticism.

1660-1850   Tucker, Martin, and others, ed.   The Critical
                        Temper; a Survey of Modern Criticism on
                        English and American Literature from the
                        Beginnings to the 20th Century.   N. Y. ,
                        Frederick Ungar, 1969.   3 vols.
                    Research compiled from scholarly and critical
                    journals of literary history and opinion, studies
                    of a writer, critical interest on a literature,
                    period or esthetic movement. Vol. 2: From
                    Milton to Romantic Literature (1600-1850).

1660-1900   Nicoll, Allardyce.   English Drama, 1600-1900.
                        Cambridge, University Press, 1952-59.
                        6 vols.
                    Covers Restoration drama through late 19th
                    century; vol. 6 is a short-title alphabetical
                    catalog of plays produced and printed in England
                    during the years covered.

1660-1932   Agate, James Evershed.   The English Dramatic
                       Critics; an Anthology, 1660-1932.   N. Y. ,
                       Hill & Wang, 1958.
                   Includes selections from Goldsmith, Addison,
                   Beerbohm, Lamb, Shaw, and others.

1668-1957   Hewitt, B. W.   Theatre U. S. A. , 1668-1957.
                       N. Y. , McGraw-Hill, 1959.
                   Contemporary accounts are used extensively in
                   this chronicle of facts and criticism.

1699-1799   Hawkins, Frederick William.   The French
                       Stage in the Eighteenth Century.   N. Y. ,
                       Greenwood Press, 1969.   2 vols.
                   A chronology of criticism of the French stage,
                   1699-1799.

1699-1894   Odell, George C. D.   Annals of the New York
                       Stage.   N. Y. , Columbia University Press,
                       1927-1945.
                   A very full account of the history of the stage
                   in New York City, covering plays, actors,
                   critics, theatres, etc. , with the historical
                   background of each period.   Covers the years
                   1699 through 1894.

1700-1799   Mantzius, Karl.   A History of Theatrical Art
                       in Ancient and Modern Times.   N. Y. ,
                       Peter Smith, 1937.   6 vols.
                   A comprehensive classical study.   Vol. 5:
                   Great Actors of the 18th Century.

1720-1800   Clark, William Smith.   The Irish Stage in the
                       Country Towns, 1720 to 1800.   Oxford,
                       Clarendon Press, 1965.
                   An account of theatricals in Ireland, continuing
                   the author's earliest volume from late Middle
                   Ages to 1720.

1732-1901   Brown, Thomas Allston.   A History of the New
                       York Stage.   N. Y. , B. Blom, 1964.   3
                       vols.
                   Covers the period from the first performance
                   in 1732 to 1901.

1733-1870   Brown, Thomas Allston.   History of the Ameri-
                       can Stage.   N. Y. , B. Franklin, 1969.
                   A standard source for plays and performances
                   from 1733 to 1870.

1800-1900   Carlson, Marvin A.   The French Stage in the
                       Nineteenth Century.   Metuchen, N. J. ,
                       Scarecrow Press, 1972.

A survey with lengthy bibliography and index
of the period 1800-1900.

1800-1900   Carlson, Marvin A. The German Stage in the
                     Nineteenth Century.   Metuchen, N. J. ,
                     Scarecrow Press, 1972.
                   A similar work to the above, but for the Ger-
                   man stage.

1800-1900   Mantzius, Karl. A History of Theatrical Art
                     in Ancient and Modern Times.   N. Y. ,
                     Peter Smith, 1937. 6 vols.
                   A comprehensive classical study. Vol. 6:
                   Classical and Romanticism, 19th Century.

1801-1910   Rowell, George. Victorian Dramatic Criticism.
                     London, Methuen, 1971.
                   Extracts of criticism arranged according to
                   various aspects of the theatrical process; se-
                   lections made on the basis of the play in per-
                   formance rather than the play as literature.
                   Dates of the reviews range from 1801-1910.

1802-1824   Hayden, John O.   The Romantic Reviewers,
                     1802-1824.   Chicago, University of Chicago
                     Press, 1969.
                   Reviews and analysis of the periodical reviews
                   of the works of Wordsworth, Coleridge, Byron,
                   Shelley, Keats, Hazlitt, Lamb, Scott, Crabbe,
                   Hunt, Southey, and Moore.

1830-1870   Reynolds, Ernest. Early Victorian Drama.
                     N. Y. , B. Blom, 1965.
                   Covers the period of 1830-1870, one of the
                   most neglected, yet vital and diverse periods
                   of English drama.

1850-1900   Tucker, Martin, and others, ed.   The Critical
                     Temper; a Survey of Modern Criticism on
                     English and American Literature from the
                     Beginnings to the 20th Century.   N. Y. ,
                     Frederick Ungar, 1969. 3 vols.
                   Research compiled from scholarly and critical
                   journals of literary history and opinion, studies
                   of a writer, critical interest on a literature,
                   period or esthetic movement; Vol. 3: Victorian
                   and American Literature (1850-1900).

1850-1950   Encyclopédie du Théâtre Contemporain, dirigée
                     par Gilles Queant avec la collaboration de
                     Frederic Towarnicki. Paris, Plaisir de
                     France, 1957. 2 vols.
                   Survey of the French theatre in text and pic-

tures, 1850-1950, with an annual chronological chart of all the theatre arts, 1880-1950.

1860-1970   Blum, Daniel.   A Pictorial History of the
                   American Theatre: 1860-1970.   3rd ed.
                   N.Y., Crown, 1969.
                   A permanent record of all the great plays and
                   players with a covering essay on the American
                   theatre before 1860, going back to 1665.

1870-1970   Brockett, Oscar G. and Robert R. Findlay.
                   Century of Innovation; A History of Euro-
                   pean and American Theatre and Drama Since
                   1870.   Englewood Cliffs, N.J., Prentice-
                   Hall, 1973.
                   A monumental concentration of the Western
                   mode from the advent of the "modern" era
                   around 1870 until the early 1970s as seen in
                   several European countries and the United
                   States.

1890-   Deutsches Bühnen-Jahrbuch; Theater Geschicht-
                   liches Jahr- und Adressenbuch.   Berlin,
                   F. A. Günther & Sohn, etc., Vol. 1,
                   1890-
                   Annual directory of German theatre; title and
                   dates of publication vary.

1890-1973   Roose-Evans, James.   Experimental Theatre
                   from Stanislavsky to Today.   Rev. ed.
                   N.Y., Universe Books, 1973.
                   Covers the important writers, directors and
                   plays of this genre (c. 1890s to date); includes
                   an index of titles criticized.

1890-1900   Clapp, John Bouve, & Edwin Francis Edgett.
                   Players of the Present.   N.Y., B. Frank-
                   lin, 1970.
                   A biographical-critical record of hundreds of
                   American performers, 1890s to 1900.

1890-1967   Kohansky, Mendel.   The Hebrew Theatre; Its
                   First Fifty Years.   N.Y., Ktav Publishing
                   House, 1969.
                   Traces the history and development of the He-
                   brew theatre since its beginnings; includes
                   milestones and list of productions in the major
                   theaters.

1894-1973   Green, Stanley.   The World of Musical Comedy.
                   3rd ed.   Cranbury, N.J., A. S. Barnes,
                   1974.
                   The story of the American musical stage as

told through the careers of its foremost composers and lyricists; valuable appendix lists
musical plays from 1894-1973, giving cast,
credits, number of performances and principal
songs for every play discussed in the book.

1900-1930   Nicoll, Allardyce. English Drama, 1900-1930;
the Beginnings of the Modern Period.
Cambridge, University Press, 1973.
A survey of English drama for the period
covered with lengthy hand-list of plays for those
years alphabetically by author; gives production
dates, theatres, nature of the piece, etc.

1900-1966   Curley, Dorothy Nyren, comp. A Library of
Literary Criticism: Modern Romance
Literatures. N. Y. , Frederick Ungar,
1967.
A guide to criticism of the more important
Romance writers from around 1900; covers
critical material from both books and periodicals, giving citations to enable the reader to go
to the original sources for further material.

1904-1968   Curley, Dorothy Nyren, and Maurice Kramer,
comp. A Library of Literary Criticism:
Modern American Literature. 4th ed.
N. Y. , Frederick Ungar, 1969. 3 vols.
Similar critical guide to the above, but coverage
is for American literature; a definitive critical
key to major 20th century American writing,
1904-1968.

1909-   Stage Year Book. London, Carson and Comer-
ford, Vol. 1, 1909?-
Annual directory of the English theatre; 1969
edition edited by A. Merryn.

1917-1941   Hirniak, Yosyp, and others. Soviet Theatres,
1917-1941; a Collection of Articles. N. Y. ,
Research Program on the U. S. S. R. , 1954.
A description of the basic theatre movements,
trends, and transformation during this period;
an index of play titles is given for those plays
discussed.

1921-1937   Gorchakov, Nikolai Aleksandrovich. The Theatre in Soviet Russia. N. Y. , Columbia
University Press, 1957.
A study of artistic criticism covering the gold-
en age, 1921-1937, and its period of decline
since 1937.

1942/43-   Annuaire du Spectacle: Théâtre, Cinéma,
                Musique, Radio, Télévision.   Paris,
                Raoult, Vol. 1, 1942/43-
                Annual directory of theatres, producers, di-
                rectors, actors, etc. in France, Belgium,
                French-speaking Switzerland.

1942-1972   Mowry, Hua-yuan Li.   Yang-Pan Hsi--New
                Theater in China.   (Studies in Chinese
                Communist Terminology no. 15.) Berkeley,
                Center for Chinese Studies, Univ. of Calif.
                Pr., 1973.
                An interpretation of some of the recent de-
                velopments in the theater in Communist China:
                social, educational, and political phenomena
                rather than merely the theater as literature and
                art; includes synopsis of development of text
                of plays.

1944/45-   Theatre World.   Philadelphia, Chilton, Vol. 1,
                1944/45-
                Edited by Daniel Blum through 1963/64, con-
                tinued by John Willis, 1964/65 to date. Covers
                the annual theatre activities in New York and
                prominent companies throughout the U.S. Gives
                credits, pictures, scenes on stage, biographical
                sketches, annual awards, and obituaries. A
                companion to Screen World.

1950-1970   Hinchliffe, Arnold P.   British Theatre, 1950-
                1970. London, Rowman & Littlefield, 1974.
                Twenty years of theatrical history from heroic
                acting, the Royal Court, theatre of the absurd,
                the producer's theatre, the living theatre.

1960-1970   Croyden, Margaret.   Lunatics, Lovers and
                Poets: the Contemporary Experimental
                Theatre.   N.Y., McGraw-Hill, 1974.
                An evaluation and description of a phenomenon
                of the 1960s--a theatre that did not depend on
                the playwright; traces historical sources of the
                movement.

1960-1973   Lesnick, Henry.   Guerilla Street Theater.
                N.Y., Bard Books, Avon, 1973.
                Survey of the radical political theater performed
                in the streets, schools, shopping centers, out-
                side plant gates--anywhere people gather; in-
                cludes criticism, synopses and scripts of sig-
                nificant performances.

1960-1973   Schevill, James.   Break Out! In Search of
                New Theatrical Environments.   Chicago,

Swallow Press, 1973.
Investigates the breakout from conventional
theatres of entertainment, particularly the
proscenium arch; trends toward more intimate
dramatic encounters indoors and outdoors; includes examples of scripts and visions for the
21st century.

1973-

Theatre Review. ed. by Eric Johns. London,
W. H. Allen, 1973-
A chronicle of the theatre in London by the
year, providing a comprehensive breakdown of
the plays which have opened May through the
following April of each year. It includes feature articles on various aspects of the theatre.
Similar in format to Film Review.

REVIEW INDEXING SERVICES

1802-1906   Poole's Index to Periodical Literature. N. Y. ,
                      Peter Smith. 1802-1906.
                Citations listed under "Drama" and "Plays. "

1890-1899   19th Century Readers' Guide to Periodical
                      Literature. N. Y. , H. W. Wilson Co. ,
                      1890-1899.
                Citations under "Dramas" and "Dramas--
                Criticism, plots. "

1896-1964   Bibliographie der Deutschen Zeitschriften-
                      literatur. (IBZ, Abt. A.) Leipzig,
                      Dietrich. N. Y. , Kraus, 1896-1964.
                Wide coverage is useful for finding materials
                in American and English periodicals as well as
                in French, Italian, and other European publi-
                cations. For dramatic criticism check under
                "Drama. " Merged into Internationale Bibli-
                ographie der Zeitschriftenliteratur.

1900-   Readers' Guide to Periodical Literature. N. Y. ,
                      H. W. Wilson Co. , 1900-
                Citations under "Drama," "Dramas," and
                "Dramatic criticism. "

1900-   Essay and General Literature Index. N. Y. ,
                      H. W. Wilson, 1900-
                Indexes essays and criticisms collected from
                books. Check under "Dramatic Criticism. "

1900-1943   Bibliographie der Rezensionen. (IBZ, Abt. C.)
                      Leipzig, Dietrich. N. Y. , Kraus, 1900-
                      1943.
                Indexes reviews of books printed in some 3,000
                German periodicals and about 2,000 periodicals
                in languages other than German. A very com-
                prehensive list, especially useful in American
                and English research libraries as it indexes
                many American and English sets not included
                in Book Review Digest. Supplements IBZ, Abt. A.

1905-   Book Review Digest. N.Y., H. W. Wilson
                         Co., 1905-
                         Includes digests of reviews of plays as litera-
                         ture after they have been published in book
                         form.   There may be a considerable time
                         lapse from the time a play is only in script or
                         acting version until it is published commercial-
                         ly.   Not all plays are included and many times
                         Readers' Guide is a better source.   Check sub-
                         ject index under "Dramas" or under the author
                         in the yearly volume in which the play was
                         first published.   The monthly issues cumulate
                         with a final bound volume each year.

1907-   Humanities Index. N.Y., H. W. Wilson Co.,
                         1974-   Formerly International Index to
                         Periodicals, 1907-1965.   Became Social
                         Sciences and Humanities Index, 1965-1973.
                         Title split into two parts in 1974.
                         Monthly cumulations with annual permanent
                         volumes.   Indexes international dramas under
                         "Dramas--Criticism," "Drama--History & Cri-
                         ticism," "Musical Comedies, Reviews--Criti-
                         cism."

1907-   Social Sciences Index. N.Y., H. W. Wilson,
                         1974-   Formerly International Index to
                         Periodicals, 1907-1965.   Became Social
                         Sciences and Humanities Index, 1965-1973.
                         Title split into two parts in 1974.
                         Monthly cumulations with annual permanent
                         volumes.   Indexes international dramas under
                         "Dramas--Criticism," "Drama--History & Cri-
                         ticism," "Musical Comedies, Revues--Criti-
                         cism."

1909-1949   Cumulated Dramatic Index. Boston, G. K.
                         Hall, 1965.   Cumulation of F. W. Faxon
                         Co.'s Dramatic Index, 1909-1949.
                         For plays check citations under individual title
                         as well as under "Dramas" by subject area.

1911-1943   Bibliographie der Fremdsprachigen Zeitschriften-
                         literatur. (IBZ, Abt. B.) Leipzig, Die-
                         trich. N.Y., Kraus, 1911-1943.
                         Indexes about 1,400 periodicals and general
                         works in the principal non-German languages.
                         For criticism of motion pictures check under
                         "Film." Merged into Internationale Bibliog-
                         raphie der Zeitschriftenliteratur.

1921-   MLA International Bibliography of Books and
                         Articles on the Modern Languages and Lit-

erature. N. Y. , Modern Language Association of America, 1921-
To find critical reviews of plays and playwrights consult table of contents each year under classification and period. Under serial
numbers given for each category, articles will
be grouped alphabetically by author being criticized.

1941-   Facts on File. N. Y. , Facts on File, 1941-
Weekly national and foreign news reference
service with cumulative index. Consult index
under "Theater--Play openings," to obtain very
short synopses of plays; gives basic credits
and opening date of plays.

1949-   Index to Religious Periodical Literature.
Chicago, American Theological Library
Association, 1949-
An author and subject index to journals in re-
ligion and related areas. Drama reviews cover
also plays with other than religious themes.
Check citations under "Dramas--Criticism of
single works," and "Religious drama."

1949-   Music Index. Detroit, Information Coordinators,
Inc. , 1949-
A subject-author guide to current music periodical literature; issued monthly with an annual cumulation. Check citations under "Drama
and music."

1957-   Guide to the Performing Arts, ed. by S. Yan-
cey Belknap. Metuchen, N. J. , Scarecrow
Press, 1957-
Annual index listing articles and illustrations
from periodicals on music, dance, theatre,
opera, films, television, and recordings. Includes history and criticism, reviews, biographical citations. Contains many entries not
covered by other indexes.

1958-   Abstracts of English Studies. Urbana, Ill. ,
National Council of Teachers of English,
Vol. 1, 1958-
Abstracts from 1,500 journals and numerous
monographs dealing with American and English
literature, and world literature in English language. Check index under "Theatre and Drama," and then "Criticism."

1960-   Index to Book Reviews in the Humanities.
Williamston, Michigan, Phillip Thomson,
1960-

Includes citations of reviews of plays as literature, indexed by author of the play. Reviews
are indexed as they appear and no attempt is
made to hold the title until all reviews are published. For this reason it is necessary to re-
fer to previous and subsequent volumes of the
index.

1962-
British Humanities Index. London, The Li-
        brary Association, 1962-
Published quarterly with annual cumulations;
superseded The Subject Index to Periodicals,
published 1915-1961. For criticism and reviews of plays and theatre check under "Theatre" for worldwide coverage.

1965-
Book Review Index. Detroit, Gale Research
        Co. , 1965-
Issued six times per year with annual cumulation. Check alphabetically under author for
citations of reviews of plays as published in
book form.

1965-
Internationale Bibliographie der Zeitschriften-
        literatur. Leipzig, Dietrich. N.Y. , Kraus,
        1965-
A subject index to world periodical literature in
German with cross references from English and
French forms. More than 7,600 periodicals are
consulted.

1974-
Theatre/Drama & Speech Index. Pleasant Hill,
        Calif. , Theatre/Drama & Speech Informa-
        tion Center, Vol. 1, 1974-
A comprehensive index to the journal literature
in both theatre and speech communication;
covers over 60 journals from 15 countries, also pamphlets, bibliographies, and other materials published by associations, institutions, and
individual theatres. A scholarly theatre research tool, includes reviews and criticism of
plays and performances.

NEWSPAPER INDEXES

1790-

Times, London. Index to the Times. 1790-
1966, 1970-
For reviews of plays check under "Theatrical
Productions. "

1851-

The New York Times Index: a Book of Record.
N. Y. , The New York Times Co. , 1851-
In this master key to the news, check under
"Theatre" for reviews of specific productions.
This is good to use for titles prior to 1870
when coverage also begins in The New York
Times Theatre Reviews, and until cumulated
volumes of that title are published.

1870-

The New York Times Theatre Reviews. N. Y. ,
New York Times, 1870-
Collection of reviews republished from The New
York Times, arranged chronologically and fully
indexed; includes out of town openings, revivals
and foreign plays, vaudeville productions, ice
shows, passion plays and operettas.   Follow-up
stories, background articles further analyze and
compare plays of the same period or genre.

1940-

New York Theatre Critics' Reviews. N. Y. ,
Critics' Theatre Reviews. Vol. 1, 1940-
Complete reprint reviews of performances of
plays as they originally appeared in the New
York City newspapers.   Issued weekly with an
annual index of play titles and credits; with a
cumulative index for 1940-1960 and 1961-1972.

1958-

Wall Street Journal Index. N. Y. , Dow Jones
& Co. , 1958-
Annual cumulation is divided into two sections:
corporate news and general news.   Check general news section under "Theatre reviews, "
and then under title of the play.

1960-

Index to The Christian Science Monitor.   Ann
Arbor, Michigan, University Microfilms,
1960-

For reviews of plays check under "Theatre"
and "Musicals" and then under individual play.

1969-   Alternative Press Index.   Toronto, Radical Re-
                    search Centre, 1969-
               An Index published quarterly to alternative and
               underground publications "which amplify the cry
               for social change and social justice." Check
               under "Theatre Reviews," then alphabetical by
               title of play for good coverage of the off-beat,
               off-Broadway type shows as well as for other
               plays.

1960-   National Observer Index.   Princeton, N.Y.,
                    Dow Jones & Co., 1969-
               Annual cumulation of the newspaper articles
               gives a one-sentence guide to the specific sub-
               ject of the articles; thus for play reviews,
               check under "Theatre," and if the article is
               about a specific play the title will be in the an-
               notation of the article.

1972-   Newspaper Index: Chicago Tribune; Los An-
                    geles Times; New Orleans Times-Picayune;
                    Washington Post.   Wooster, Ohio, Bell &
                    Howell, Micro Photo Division, June 1972-
               A combined index of the four named newspapers.
               Check under "Plays and Theatricals."

DRAMATIC CRITICISM CHECKLISTS

5th c. B.C.   Gwinup, Thomas, and Fidelia Dickinson.
Greek and Roman Authors: a Checklist of
Criticism. Metuchen, N. J. , Scarecrow
Press, 1973.
An index to nearly 4,000 items of recent criti-
cism of the authors of belles-lettres of ancient
Greece and Rome.

1559-1900   Arnott, James F. and John W. Robinson.
English Theatrical Literature, 1559-1900.
London, The Society for Theatre Research,
1970.
A bibliography covering general history, background material, theory and criticism in books
and periodicals.

1798-1820   Ward, William S. Literary Reviews in British
Periodicals, 1798-1820. N. Y. , Garland
Pub. Co. , 1972. 2 vols.
Contains a section of articles on drama and
theatre.

1890-1969   Palmer, Helen H. , and Jane A. Dyson, ed.
American Drama Criticism: Interpreta-
tions, 1890-1965 Inclusive, of American
Drama Since the First Play Produced in
America. Hamden, Conn. , Shoe String
Press, 1967. Supplement, 1970.
Sources of critical articles in books, peri-
odicals, and monographs; a supplementary
volume covers 1966-1969.

1900-1969   Palmer, Helen H. , and Anne J. Dyson, comp.
European Drama Criticism. Hamden,
Conn. , Shoe String Press, 1968. Supplement, 1970.
Comprehensive listing of criticism which has
appeared in books and periodicals in English
and foreign languages from 1900 to 1966. A
supplement carries the bibliography forward
through 1969.

1900-1967   Adelman, Irving, and Rita Dworkin, ed.
                 Modern Drama: a Checklist of Critical
                 Literature on 20th Century Plays.   Me-
                 tuchen, N. J. , Scarecrow Press, 1967.
                 A survey of literary criticism of drama since
                 1900 from periodicals; arranged by author and
                 title of play.

1900-1972   Breed, Paul F. and Florence M. Sniderman.
                 Dramatic Criticism Index.   Detroit, Gale
                 Research Co. , 1972.
                 A bibliography of commentaries on playwrights
                 from Ibsen to the avant-garde taken from ap-
                 proximately 630 books and over 200 periodicals,
                 the majority of them from the 20th Century and
                 some from 19th Century playwrights still being
                 performed.

1909-1963   Salem, James M.   A Guide to Critical Reviews.
                 Metuchen, N. J. , Scarecrow Press, 1966-
                 1973.   4 pts. in 5 vols.
                 A list of sources of critical reviews in peri-
                 odicals: Part I: American Drama from
                 O'Neill to Albee, 1909-1969.   1973.   Part II:
                 The Musical from Rodgers & Hart to Lerner
                 & Loewe.   1967.   Part III: British and Con-
                 tinental Drama from Ibsen to Pinter.   1968.
                 Part IV: The Screenplay from "The Jazz Sing-
                 er" to "Dr. Strangelove," 1927-1963.   2 vols.
                 1971.

1940-1946   Coleman, Arthur, and Gary R. Tyler, ed.
                 Drama Criticism: a Checklist of Inter-
                 pretation Since 1940 of English and Ameri-
                 can Plays.   Denver, Alan S. Swallow, 1966.
                 A checklist of criticism published in books and
                 periodicals from 1940 to 1946.

1951-   Kosch, Wilhelm.   Deutsches Theaterlexikon.
                 Klagenfurt, Kleinmayr, 1951-
                 Bio-bibliographical information on persons, his-
                 tory, theories, themes, criticism from news-
                 papers, periodicals and books.

1972-   Chicorel Bibliography to the Performing Arts,
                 ed. by Marietta Chicorel.   (Chicorel Index
                 Series Vol. 3A.) N. Y. , Chicorel Library
                 Pub. Corp. , 1972.
                 A guide to more than 8,000 entries arranged un-
                 der more than 300 subject headings.   The sec-
                 tion on history and criticism is arranged by
                 country and chronological period.

COLLECTED REVIEWS OF INDIVIDUAL CRITICS

5th c. B. C.
-1960
Altshuler, Thelma, and Richard Paul Janaro. Responses to Drama; an Introduction to Plays and Movies. N. Y., Houghton Mifflin, 1967.
The purpose of this book is to assist playgoers (or readers) and film viewers in making evaluations; in so doing, presents choice excerpts from reviews, opinions on criticism by critics, craft of the theatre and film, and a chronology of theatre and film from the Age of Pericles (5th Century) to Fellini's "La Dolce Vita" (1960).

5th c. B. C.
-1964
Mabley, Edward. Dramatic Construction; an Outline of Basic Principles. N. Y., Chilton Book Co., 1972.
Gives technical analyses of 24 famous plays from "Oedipus the King" (c. 427 B. C.) to "Marat/Sade" (1964), including one film: "Citizen Kane."

1660-1932
Agate, James. The English Dramatic Critics; an Anthology, 1660-1932. N. Y., Hill and Wang, 1958.
Collected dramatic criticism of Addison, Steele, Goldsmith, Boswell, Lamb, Shaw, and others as appeared in various newspapers and publications during the period stated. An index provides titles of plays criticized.

1752-1934
Moses, Montrose J. The American Theatre as Seen by Its Critics, 1752-1934. N. Y., Cooper Square Pub., 1934.
A collection of dramatic criticism covering 182 years; includes biographical sketches and a storehouse of information on the American plays and playwrights.

1868-1883
Cook, Edward Dutton. Nights at the Play: a View of the English Stage. London, Chatto & Windus, 1883. N. Y., Blom, 1970. 2 vols.

Theatrical reviews contributed to Pall Mall
Gazette and World Newspaper, 1868-1883.

1893-1897   Archer, William. The Theatrical World of
               1893-1897. N. Y. , B. Blom, 1971. 5 vols.
               Annual review of the British stage with critical
               reviews by Archer as they appeared in World,
               Pall Mall, Budget and New Budget; includes
               synopsis of plays, performances, dates, thea-
               tres, and casts for the plays of the year.

1895-1898   Shaw, George Bernard. Dramatic Opinions and
               Essays. N. Y. , Brentano's, 1907. 2 vols.
               Shaw's dramatic criticisms which appeared in
               Saturday Review (London), beginning Jan. 5,
               1895 and ending May 21, 1898.

1898-1903   Beerbohm, Max. More Theatres, 1898-1903.
               N. Y. , Taplinger, 1969.
               More play reviews published in Saturday Review
               (London) during the above years.

1898-1911   Beerbohm, Max. Around Theatres, 1898-1911.
               N. Y. , Taplinger, 1969.
               A collection of 153 play reviews which appeared
               in Saturday Review (London) during the above
               years.

1900-1968   O'Driscoll, Robert, ed. Theatre and National-
               ism in Twentieth-century Ireland. Toronto,
               University of Toronto Press, 1971.
               A collection of papers on Irish theatre read at
               the second inter-university Seminar in Irish
               Studies, 1968; plays and playwrights covered
               from 1900.

1900-1970   Atkinson, Justin Brooks. Atkinson's Broad-
               way. N. Y. , Macmillan, 1971.
               History and criticism of the Broadway theatre
               from the turn of the century to 1971.

1904-1910   Beerbohm, Max. Last Theatres, 1904-1910.
               N. Y. , Taplinger, 1970.
               The remaining play reviews published in
               Saturday Review (London) for the years above.

1917-1967   Toohey, John L. A History of the Pulitzer
               Prize Plays. N. Y. , Citadel Press, 1967.
               Traces history and gives highlights of reviews
               of the winning plays and runner-ups since the
               first award, 1917/1918; includes the Theatre
               Critics Circle Awards, which began in 1936.

1918-1922   Woollcott, Alexander. Shouts and Murmurs;
                        Echoes of a Thousand and One First Nights.
                        N. Y. , Century Co. , 1922.
                   Early reviews and reminiscences of plays,
                   players, and the theatre.

1919-1929   Eaton, Walter Prichard. Theatre Guild, the
                        First 10 Years. N. Y. , Brentano's, 1929.
                   Historical account of the plays and productions
                   with articles by the directors of the produc-
                   tions of The Guild, 1919-1929.

1920-1947   Young, Stark. Immortal Shadows; a Book of
                        Dramatic Criticism. N. Y. , Hill & Wang,
                        1948.
                   Play reviews from The New Republic, Theatre
                   Arts, and New York Times, during the period
                   of the early 1920s through 1947.

1926-1967   Hogan, Robert. After the Irish Renaissance;
                        a Critical History of the Irish Drama since
                        "The Plough and the Stars. " Minneapolis,
                        University of Minnesota Press, 1967.
                   A critical account of Irish dramatic writing
                   since 1926.

1928-1939   Waldau, Roy S. Vintage Years of the Theatre
                        Guild. Cleveland, Case Western Reserve
                        University, 1972.
                   Covers plays, performances, casts, critics'
                   reviews of productions of The Guild, 1928-
                   1939.

1928-1938   Brown, John Mason. Two on the Aisle: 10
                        Years of the American Theatre in Per-
                        formance. Port Washington, N. Y. , Ken-
                        nikat Press, 1938.
                   Reprints of his reviews written for the New
                   York Post, 1928-1938.

1920-1960   Brown, John Mason. Dramatis Personae; a
                        Retrospective Show. N. Y. , Viking, 1963.
                   Selections of his writing as a critic of Theatre
                   Arts, New York Post, New York World Tele-
                   gram, and Saturday Review, from the 1920s
                   to 1960s.

1935-1947   Atkinson, Justin Brooks. Broadway Scrapbook.
                        N. Y. , Theatre Arts, 1947.
                   Atkinson's play reviews as published in The
                   New York Times, 1935-1947.

1935-1966   Gassner, John. Dramatic Soundings: Evalu-

ations and Retractions Culled from 30
Years of Dramatic Criticism.   N. Y.,
Crown, 1968.
Critical essays on plays from 1935 to 1966.

1938-1940   Brown, John Mason.   Broadway in Review.
N. Y., W. W. Norton, 1940; Books for Libraries, 1969.
Essays and reviews of Broadway plays, 1938-
40.

1940-1964   Freedman, Morris, ed.   Essays in the Modern
Drama.   Boston, Heath, 1964.
Drama criticism as literature rather than per-
formance; a collection of writings from the
1940s through 1964, by Mencken, Shaw, Stark
Young, John Gassner, Walter Kerr, Martin
Esslin, and others, on master playwrights from
Ibsen to Pinter.

1944-1956   Bentley, Eric.   What Is Theatre?   N. Y.,
Atheneum, 1968.
Incorporates his The Dramatic Event and other
reviews, 1944-1967, the majority of which were
originally published in The New Republic, 1952-
1956.

1945-1954   Bentley, Eric.   The Dramatic Event; an American Chronicle.   N. Y., Horizon Press,
1954.
Contains more than 50 periodical essays on international theatre.

1947-1957   Clurman, Harold.   Lies Like Truth: Theatre
Reviews and Essays.   N. Y., Macmillan,
1958.
Reviews as published in Tomorrow Magazine,
The New Republic, and The Nation, 1947-1957.

1950-1959   Duprey, Richard A.   Just Off the Aisle; the
Ramblings of a Catholic Critic.   West-
minister, Maryland, The Newman Press,
1962.
Criticism of plays and films from a Catholic
viewpoint; articles appeared in The Critic, The
Catholic Standard and Times, mostly during
the 1950s.

1950-1973   Esslin, Martin, The Theatre of the Absurd.
Rev. ed. Woodstock, N. Y., Overlook
Press, 1973.
Covers the expressionist type of drama during
the 1950s and 1960s with update to 1973, from
Ionesco, Beckett, Camus, Pinter and others.

1951-1960   Tynan, Kenneth. Curtains; Selections from the
                        Drama Criticism and Related Writings.
                        N. Y. , Atheneum, 1961.
                   Theatre criticism written from 1951 to 1960 as
                   published in various English and American peri-
                   odicals, arranged chronologically and geograph-
                   ically.

1957-1967   Tynan, Kenneth. Tynan Right & Left: Plays,
                        Films, People, Places and Events.   N. Y. ,
                        Atheneum, 1967.
                   Critical pieces written from 1957 to 1967 of
                   plays and films including other performing arts,
                   public spectacles and events, places and peo-
                   ple.   Check index for titles of plays and films
                   criticized.

1959-1965   Brustein, Robert. Seasons of Discontent.
                        N. Y. , Simon & Schuster, 1965.
                   Review articles from The New Republic, 1959-
                   1965.

1960-1970   McCrindle, Joseph F. , comp.   Behind the
                        Scenes; Theater and Film Interviews from
                        the Transatlantic Review.   N. Y. , Holt,
                        Rinehart & Winston, 1971.
                   Discussion on contemporary theater and films
                   with Inge, Quintero, Marcel Marceau, Tony
                   Richardson, Gore Vidal, Jules Feiffer, Edward
                   Albee, Joan Littlewood, Federico Fellini, Alan
                   Schneider, and others.   These articles original-
                   ly appeared in the Transatlantic Review, Lon-
                   don, in the '60s and early '70s.

1960-1971   Gilliatt, Penelope. Unholy Fools; Wits, Com-
                        ics, Disturbers of the Peace: Film &
                        Theater. N. Y. , Viking Press, 1973.
                   A collection of writings on films and the thea-
                   tre which originally appeared in The Guardian,
                   Harpers, Queen, The New Yorker, The Ob-
                   server, Spectator, and Vogue, 1960-1971.

1961-1968   Esslin, Martin. Reflections; Essays on Modern
                        Theatre. N. Y. , Doubleday, 1968.
                   Compilation of articles, prefaces to anthologies,
                   interviews, from 1961 to 1968, on plays and
                   their productions from Ibsen through Pirandello
                   to Brecht to Ionesco, May Frisch and Peter
                   Weiss, and others.

1961-1970   Gilman, Richard. Common and Uncommon
                        Masks: Writings on Theatre.   N. Y. ,
                        Random House, 1971.

A collection of short reviews from Common-
weal, New Republic, and Newsweek, 1961-1971.

1961-1971   Lahr, John. Up Against the Fourth Wall: Es-
                     says on Modern Theatre. N.Y., Grove
                     Press, 1971.
                 A collection of essays from Evergreen Review,
                 analyzing some of the major plays of the past
                 decade.

1962-1972   Gautier, Jean Jacques. Théâtre d'Aujourd'hui:
                     Dix ans de critique dramatique et des en-
                     tretiens. Paris, Julliard, 1972.
                 Covers 10 years of criticism of the French
                 stage.

1963-1969   Gottfried, Martin. Opening Nights; Theatre
                     Criticism of the Sixties. N.Y., Putnam,
                     1969.
                 Play reviews covering the years 1963-1969
                 from New York to Europe to resident theatre
                 companies.

1964-1969   Kerr, Walter. Thirty Plays Hath November;
                     Pain and Pleasure in the Contemporary
                     Theatre. N.Y., Simon & Schuster, 1969.
                 Five years of critical drama reviews as pub-
                 lished in New York Herald Tribune and The
                 New York Times.

1967-1968   Goldman, William. The Season; a Candid Look
                     at Broadway. N.Y., Harcourt, Brace,
                     1969.
                 An evaluation of the productions of the New York
                 City stage during 1967-68.

1967-1972   Lahr, John. Astonish Me; Adventures in Con-
                     temporary Theater. N.Y., Viking Press,
                     1973.
                 A collection of pieces on pageants, playwrights,
                 and performances which originally appeared in
                 The Evergreen Review, The Village Voice, The
                 Drama Review, and Performance, late 1960s
                 and early 1970s.

LEADING THEATRE PERIODICALS

1877-1897   Theatre. London, Wyman & Sons, Vol. 1,
                        1877-1897. 42 vols.
                   Dramatic criticism, biographies, reviews of
                   the London stage; contains quality portraits of
                   the players.

1900-1931   The Theatre. N. Y. , Meyer Bros. , & Co. ,
                        Vol. 1, 1900-1931. Title changed to Thea-
                        tre Magazine, 1924. 53 vols.
                   Profusion of illustrated articles about plays and
                   players, primarily on the New York stage.
                   The index has a title section of play reviews.

1908-1929   The Mask, ed. by Edward Gordon Craig.
                        Florence, Arena Goldoni, Vol. 1-15, 1908-
                        1929. B. Blom, 1966.
                   Considered by many to be the most profound
                   writing on the theatre in the 20th Century.
                   Covering the presentation of plays from all
                   periods and countries, Craig presents his the-
                   ories on acting, directing, scene design, stage
                   managing, and criticism; the art of the theatre
                   being a combination of all these elements with
                   no one being any more important than the other.

1916-1963   Theatre Arts. N.Y., Theatre Arts, Vol. 1-47,
                        1916-1963.
                   Best periodical coverage of the period for critical
                   reviews, theatre history, design, lighting, and all
                   other facets of the legitimate theatre as an art form.

1925-   The New Yorker. N. Y. , New Yorker Maga-
                        zine, Vol. 1, 1925-
                   General sophisticated magazine of the arts,
                   music, literature, political scene, humor, but
                   with strong coverage of reviews of plays and
                   films. Check weekly for new openings. For
                   older issues consult Music Index and Readers'
                   Guide to Periodical Literature.

1934/35-   The Playbill. N. Y. , The New York Theatre
                        Program Corporation, 1934/35-

The program of the New York legitimate stage,
published weekly; uniform in size, format ad-
vertising and features, for all legitimate theatres in New York.   An important feature is
"Who's Who in the Cast," giving biographical
data for members of the cast for each play.

1935-   Cue. N.Y., Cue Pub. Co., 1935-
                     Weekly magazine guide to New York city with
                     good coverage of reviews of theatre, movies, &
                     television.

1942-   Revista de Teatro.   Rio de Janeiro, Sociedad
                        Brasileira de Autores Teatrais, No. 1,
                        1942-
                     Covers the Brazilian theatrical scene; includes
                     complete playscripts.

1946-   Sipario: Il Mensile Italiano Dello Spettacolo.
                        Rome, No. 1, 1946-
                     Covers the theatre, cinema, television, opera
                     and dance scene in Rome; includes complete
                     playscripts.

1946-   Theater der Zeit.   Berlin, East Germany,
                        Organ of Verbandes der Theaterschaffenden,
                        1946-
                     Monthly publication reviewing the performing
                     arts as well as books in these fields; includes
                     complete playscripts of plays international in
                     scope.

1949-   L'Avant-Scène du Théâtre.   Paris. No. 1,
                        1949-   Title change from L'Avant-Scène
                        Femina Théâtre.
                     Reviews plays, giving biographical information
                     on the authors, stills, casts, interviews; in-
                     cludes complete playscripts in an international
                     coverage; issued twice per month.

1952-   Italian Theatre Review.   Rome, Italian Theatre
                        Guild, 1952-
                     Quarterly publication contains play reviews,
                     gives credits, performances, theatres; outlines
                     each theatrical season; includes complete play-
                     scripts in both Italian and English.

1953-   Plays and Players.   London, Hansom Books,
                        Vol. 1, 1953-
                     Covers the theatrical scene in London and other
                     areas with reviews, criticism, stills, book re-
                     views; a companion to Films and Filming; con-
                     tains complete playscripts; issued monthly.

1955-   The Drama Review (formerly TDR, Tulane
                               Drama Review. New Orleans, Tulane Uni-
                               versity). N.Y., New York University,
                               1955-
                               Quarterly publication contains complete scripts
                               of new plays, translations, criticism, theory,
                               reviews and interviews on the theatre.

1960-   Theater Heute. Hannover, Germany, Erhard
                               Friedrich Verlag, 1960-
                               Monthly publication reviewing the performing
                               arts; includes complete playscripts.

1961-   Performing Arts in Canada. Toronto, Canadian
                               Stage and Arts Publications, Vol. 1, 1961-
                               Quarterly publication covering the theatrical
                               scene in Canada; includes complete playscripts.

1962-   Los Angeles Times Calendar. Los Angeles
                               Times.
                               Weekly magazine included in the Sunday edition
                               of the Los Angeles Times, began as a separate
                               magazine in 1962; covers events with particular-
                               ly good reviews and criticism of films, plays,
                               music, and art. Check weekly issues for new
                               openings and also short synopsis of current
                               titles playing. For back issues check News-
                               paper Index.

1968-   Yale/Theatre. New Haven, Conn., Yale Uni-
                               versity, School of Drama, No. 1, 1968-
                               Quarterly publication contains complete scripts
                               of new plays, reviews plays, films, and books
                               about the performing arts.

1971-   Performance. N.Y., Performance Foundation,
                               Inc., Vol. 1, 1971-
                               Quarterly publication containing essays, re-
                               views and criticism of plays, films and books;
                               contains complete playscripts and occasional
                               screenplays, radio and television scripts, and
                               music.

1971-   Theatre Quarterly. London, TQ Publications,
                               Ltd., Vol. 1, 1971-
                               Contains articles on theatre history, criticism,
                               reviews, and synopses of plays.

1974-   Theatrefacts: International Theatre Reference.
                               London, TQ Publications, Ltd., Vol. 1,
                               1974-
                               Covers events by country, giving reference
                               material for both practical and archival use;

includes short reviews of plays, interviews,
checklists of works of playwrights with synopsis and other information of each play; a companion to Theatre Quarterly.

LEADING REFERENCE GUIDES

Bates, Alfred, ed. The Drama: Its History, Literature, and Influence on Civilization. London, Smart and Stanley, 1903-1904.
22 vols.
Spans the broadest spectrum of the world's dramatic literature; offers detailed biography and criticism of major and minor figures
from the beginning through the 19th Century.

Baugh, Albert C. A Literary History of England. 2nd ed. N.Y.,
Appleton-Century-Crofts, 1967.
Comprehensive history of the literature of England from the Old
English period to the present; includes thorough survey of the
drama during each historical period.

Berthold, Margot. A History of World Theater. N.Y., Frederick
Ungar, 1972.
A panoramic survey of the origins and development of world theater
from the primitive theater to the present; includes extensive index
and separate bibliographies for each historical period; illustrated.

Cleaver, James. Theatre through the Ages. N.Y., Hart Pub. Co.,
1967.
A concise coverage of basic information from the Greek theatre to
the American theatre, 1966; grouped chronologically, giving major
periods, trends, plays, playwrights.

Crowell's Handbook of Contemporary Drama, by Michael Anderson
and others. N.Y., Thomas Y. Crowell, 1971.
A convenient guide to developments in the drama in Europe and the
Americas since World War II, with the emphasis on written drama,
not on theater.

Gassner, John, and Edward Quinn, ed. The Reader's Encyclopedia
of World Drama. N.Y., Thomas Y. Crowell, 1969.
A master study of drama as literature, not as theater; an encyclopedic arrangement of critical studies of plays and playwrights; contains an appendix of basic documents in dramatic theory from Aris-
totle to Dürrenmatt. The work gives critiques from every creative
nation and all areas as well as theories and trends, genres and
terminology.

Geisinger, Marion. Plays, Players, & Playwrights. N.Y., Hart
Pub. Co., 1971.

An illustrated history of the theatre chronologically arranged from
the time of the Greeks and Romans to the 20th Century (1971); an
unusually good collection of photographs and drawings accompanies
the text.

Gillie, Christopher. Longman Companion to English Literature.
    London, Longman, 1972.
Basic coverage in two main sections: Essay section, political history and institutions of England: 1066 to present day; Reference
section, an encyclopedic arrangement of names, terms, genres.
A section on drama in Britain covers 1350-1965.

Hart, James D. The Oxford Companion to American Literature.
    4th ed. N.Y., Oxford Univ. Press, 1965.
An alphabetic arrangement of scholarly short biographies, brief
bibliographies of American authors, with information regarding their
style and subjects; summaries of important American novels, stories, essays, poems, plays, etc.

Hartnoll, Phyllis, ed. The Oxford Companion to the Theatre. 3d
    ed. London, Oxford University Press, 1967.
Provides information on every aspect of the theatre up to the end
of 1964, and beyond that for England, France, and America; all
ages and all countries.

Harvey, Sir Paul. Oxford Companion to English Literature. 4th
    ed. Oxford, Clarendon Press, 1967.
A dictionary of brief articles on authors, literary works, characters
in fiction, drama, etc.

Literary History of the United States. 4th ed., N.Y., Macmillan,
    1974. 3 vols.
Comprehensive history and bibliography from Colonial times to the
present; contains basic articles on the development of drama in
America.

McGraw-Hill Encyclopedia of World Drama. N.Y., McGraw-Hill
    Book Co., 1972. 4 vols.
An international reference work which brings into focus the accomplishments of the world's dramatists, ranging from the ancient
writings of the Greeks and Romans to the twentieth century. It
presents factual information and critical evaluations of each dramatist's work and stature, biographies, synopses of plays, listing of
entire body of dramatic writings of the dramatists, and bibliographies.

Matlaw, Myron. Modern World Drama; an Encyclopedia. N.Y.,
    Dutton, 1972.
Covers the work of all major 19th Century playwrights who lived
into this century, as well as the work of all notable 20th Century
playwrights up to the present time; a comprehensive reference in a
single alphabetical listing of plays, playwrights, countries, and
technical terms; gives synopses of plays and information on their
production.

Melchinger, Siegfried. The Concise Encyclopedia of Modern Drama.
    N.Y., Horizon Press, 1964.
Covers drama from Ibsen to Beckett; documents on contemporary
playwriting; glossary of modern dramatic theory; biographies of
playwrights; chronology of first performances, 1900-1964; bibliography; illustrated with scenes from productions.

Pride, Leo B., ed. International Theatre Directory; A World Di-
    rectory of the Theatre and Performing Arts. N.Y., Simon
    and Schuster, 1973.
A theatre directory listing by country, cities and towns, giving address, pertinent information, and a covering essay about each country's performing arts; includes photographs of the theatre buildings
and statistical information.

The Reader's Encyclopedia of American Literature, by Max J.
    Herzberg. N.Y., Thomas Y. Crowell, 1962.
Comprehensive dictionary of American authors, critics, literary
movements, synopsis of books and plays, characters; more inclusive
than Oxford Companion to American Literature.

Rigdon, Walter, ed. The Biographical Encyclopedia & Who's Who
    of the American Theatre. N.Y., James H. Heineman, 1966.
The single most complete work on the American theatre; contains
alphabetical listing of productions presented in New York City from
Jan. 1, 1900 through May 31, 1964; complete playbills 1959 to 1964
covering New York City and leading experimental and repertory theatre groups throughout the United States; biographical who's who;
theatre groups and theatre buildings; awards; bibliography; discog-
raphy; necrology.

Webster's New World Companion to English and American Literature,
    ed. by Arthur Pollard, N.Y., World Publishing, 1973.
Encyclopedic arrangement of authors giving biographical material and
works; genres; bibliography.

Who's Who in the Theatre; a Biographical Record of the Contemporary
    Stage. 15th ed. N.Y., Pitman Pub. Corp., 1972.
Besides biographical and career information on players, directors,
composers, and other theatre notables, contains London playbills,
1921-1965, 1966-1970; New York playbills, 1966-1970; long runs,
principal theatres in London and New York and other information.

PLAY SYNOPSES AND
PRODUCTION CONTROLLING AGENCIES

Synopses

2500 B.C.- 1959 A.D.	Sobel, Bernard. <u>New Theatre Handbook and</u> <u>Digest of Plays</u>. 3rd ed. N.Y., Crown, 1959. Contains short but terse digests and informa- tion on plays from all periods and all countries from the earliest times, for example, Abydos Passion Play, (2500 B.C.); articles under Drama and Theatre headings are arranged chronologically within the national sections; contains a section under Drama, Subjects, which lists plays by type of subject matter.
5th c. B.C.- 1950s	National Council of Teachers of English. Com- mittee on Playlist. <u>Guide to Play Selection</u>. 2nd ed., N.Y. Appleton-Century-Crofts, 1958. Designed to assist directors of theatre groups in the selection of plays for production. Be- ginning with Greek and Roman drama, then Medieval and Renaissance plays, plays from 1650 to 1870, and modern plays, one-act plays, television plays, gives summary, number of sets, period, controlling agency and royalty.
5th c. B.C.- mid-20th c.	Plummer, Gail. <u>Dramatists' Guide to Selec-</u> <u>tion of Plays and Musicals</u>. Dubuque, Iowa, W. C. Brown Co., 1963. Assists in play selection by listing plays by type; gives cast and set requirements, royalty and other information; includes synopses of plays. A wide coverage includes classics, manuscript plays, musical comedies and one- act plays from the Greeks through mid-20th Century.
5th c. B.C.- 1970	Grumbach, Jane and Robert Emerson. <u>Actors</u> <u>Guide to Monologues</u>. N.Y., Drama Book Specialists, 1972.

Contains directions to 700 monologues from all
periods from the Greeks to modern plays. Useful for auditions and classwork, each entry
lists the title and author of the play, the char-
acter's name and age, approximate time of
performance, the first line of the speech, and
the act and scene in which it appears. The
entries are grouped by classical, modern,
male, female, serious, comic, and serio-
comic.

5th c. B.C.-   Koehmstedt, Carol L.   Plot Summary Index.
20th c.   Metuchen, N.J., Scarecrow Press, 1973.
                     An index to plots, outlines, and synopses in
                     compilations; includes plays from the Greeks
                     to the present.

492 B.C.-   Shipley, Joseph T.   Guide to Great Plays.
20th c.   Washington, D.C., Public Affairs Press,
                          1956.
                     For each play the following information is
                     given: author, dates, national origin, synop-
                     sis, important aspects of the play's history,
                     first performance and other notable produc-
                     tions, analysis of significant aspects of the
                     play, opinions of critics and reviewers, and
                     prominent players who have acted in the plays.

472 B.C.-   Shank, Theodore Junior, ed.   Digest of 500
1956   Plays. N.Y., Collier, 1963.
                     Gives plot outlines and production notes select-
                     ed from all periods and all countries; includes
                     controlling agency and royalty for performance
                     rights information.

411 B.C.-   Cartmell, Van Henry.   Plot Outlines of 100
1935 A.D.   Famous Plays.   Philadelphia, Blakiston
                          Co., 1945.
                     Representative plays of a people and an era,
                     these outlines cover all periods and countries
                     from the Greeks and Romans to "Life with
                     Father." The sequence is roughly chronologi-
                     cal in reverse order and in each group the
                     most recent play is given first.

1500-1890   Hazlitt, W. Carew.   A Manual for the Col-
                          lector and Amateur of Old English Plays.
                          London, Pickering & Chatto, 1892. John-
                          son reprint, 1967.
                     A title index of old English plays from c. 1500
                     to 1890 giving author, date, synopsis, histori-
                     cal facts about the plays and productions. A
                     name index giving theatres and theatrical com-
                     panies is included.

1595-1971   Butler, Ivan. The 100 Best Full-Length Plays
     for Amateurs. London, Pelham Books,
     1972.
     The outline of each play is given, author, pub-
     lisher or controlling agency, cast, number of
     sets required, and period; ranges from Shake-
     speare to the present.

1600-1970   Grumbach, Jane and Robert Emerson. Actors
     Guide to Scenes. N.Y., Drama Book
     Specialists, 1973.
     Contains directions to 600 scenes from pub-
     lished plays; each entry lists title, author,
     character's name, sex, and age, approximate
     time of the performance, first line of the
     scene, and act and scene in which it appears;
     publishers and controlling agencies are given.
     Although the emphasis is on modern plays,
     Shakespearean scenes and other early works
     are included. It is a companion to Actors
     Guide to Monologues.

1600-1970   Grumbach, Jane and Robert Emerson. More
     Actors Guide to Monologues. N.Y., Drama
     Book Specialists, 1974.
     A second collection indexing sources to mono-
     logues; similar to the first collection, it gives
     play title, author, character and age, per-
     formance time, act and scene, first line and
     page number of the scene. This collection
     features mainly modern monologues; however,
     a number of early works are included, such as
     Molière and Beaumarchais.

1766-1959   Lovell, John. Digest of Great American Plays.
     N.Y., Thomas Y. Crowell Co., 1961.
     Contains complete summaries to more than 100
     plays dating from 1766 to 1959, representing
     works by every major writer and many minor
     writers; offers a comprehensive sampling of
     dramatic literature that has been unjustly neg-
     lected. It attempts to reproduce not only the
     story but the flavor, the mood and the dramatic
     essence of each play and its characters; ana-
     lyzes the basic components of each play:
     theme, plot, characters, probable goals of the
     author, social and cultural characteristics.

1860-1960   Sprinchorn, Evert, ed. 20th Century Plays in
     Synopsis. N.Y., T. Y. Crowell, 1965.
     Gives act-by-act summaries of representative
     dramas, 1860-1960; includes biographical notes
     on the playwrights.

40   PLAYS

1860-1970   Ewen, David. New Complete Book of the
                        American Musical Theater. N.Y., Holt,
                        Rinehart & Winston, 1970.
                     Alphabetical arrangement of titles gives credits,
                     dates, runs, synopsis, critical excerpts from
                     reviews of the period from 1860 through 1970.

1894-   Best Plays. N.Y., Dodd, Mead, 1894-
                     A comprehensive coverage of activities of each
                     theatrical season in New York with summaries
                     of other regions. Gives digests of the play-
                     scripts with key scenes and summaries of other
                     scenes; includes pertinent statistics and other
                     information on each play.

1894-1971   Guernsey, Otis L. Jr., comp. Directory of
                        the American Theater, 1894-1971. N.Y.,
                        Dodd, Mead, 1971.
                     An index to the complete series above giving
                     titles, authors, and composers of Broadway,
                     Off-Broadway, and Off Off-Broadway shows and
                     their sources.

1894-1973   Green, Stanley. The World of Musical Comedy.
                        3rd ed. Cranbury, N.J., A. S. Barnes,
                        1974.
                     The story of the American musical stage as
                     told through the careers of its foremost com-
                     posers and lyricists, giving casts, credits,
                     synopses, criticism, number of performances
                     and principal songs for plays produced 1894-
                     1973.

1942/43-   The Theatre Book of the Year; a record and
  1950/51   an interpretation by George Jean Nathan.
                        N.Y., Knopf, 1942/43-1950/51.
                     A statistical record and critical interpretation
                     of the plays produced annually in the American
                     Theatre.

1945-1970   Siegfried, Kienzle. Modern World Theater; a
                        guide to productions in Europe and the U.S.
                        since 1945. N.Y., Frederick Ungar Pub.,
                        1970.
                     578 plays are discussed, giving author, dates,
                     national origin, first performance, etc.

1949/1952-   Play Index. N.Y., H. W. Wilson Co., 1949/
                        52-
                     Indexes plays in collections with an author,
                     title, and subject approach; gives very brief
                     annotations as to plot; number of characters,
                     number of sets, cast analysis; directory of

publishers and controlling agencies for production.

1957-1959   Broadway's Best, edited by John Chapman.
             N.Y., Doubleday, 1957-1959.
             A complete record of the theatrical year with
             critical and statistical survey; gives synopses
             of the plays, casts, dates of performances,
             etc.

1960-1973   Lesnick, Henry. Guerilla Street Theatre.
             N.Y., Bard Books, Avon, 1973.
             Survey of the radical political theater per-
             formed in the streets, schools, shopping cen-
             ters, outside plant gates--anywhere people
             gather; includes criticism, synopses and scripts
             of significant performances.

1969-   Wright, Edward A. and Lenthiel H. Downs.
             A Primer for Playgoers. 2d ed. Engle-
             wood Cliffs, N.J., 1969.
             Introduces the playgoer to the audience, the
             script, the production, the technicians, the
             dramatic criticism; includes synopses of plays,
             short scenes from plays, and excerpts from
             professional critics.

1974-   Cameron, Kenneth M. and Theodore J. C.
             Hoffman. A Guide to Theatre Study. 2nd
             ed. N.Y., Macmillan, 1974.
             A basic guide for students in introductory thea-
             tre built around discussions within a historical
             context; gives synopsis and excerpts from se-
             lected plays that represent major periods and
             types.

Controlling Agencies

Baker's Plays. Boston, Walter H. Baker Co.
Annual catalog of plays controlled by the publisher which was established in 1934. Gives synopses of plays, type of casts required,
source of plots, capsule comments from the press, production
rights, and fees for royalties and scripts.
Address: 100 Chauncy St.
         Boston, Mass.   02111

Dramatic Publishing Company Catalog of Plays and Musical Comedies. Chicago, The Company.
Annual catalog of plays controlled by the company founded by

Charles H. Sergel in 1885. Gives synopses of plays, type of casts required, source of plots, fees for royalties and scripts. Many of the plays are specially written from famous novels, short stories, and popular films and musicals.
Address: 86 E. Randolph Street
          Chicago, Ill. 60601

Dramatist Play Service Complete Catalog of Plays. N.Y., The
    Service.
Annual cumulation of plays controlled by the service which was started by Barrett H. Clark in 1936. Gives synopses of plays, type of casts required, source of plots, few lines from reviews. Fees for royalties and scripts including unpublished plays in manuscript and included.
Address: 440 Park Avenue South
          New York, N.Y. 10016

Century Library, Inc., and Select Theatre Corp., 234 West 44th
    Street, New York, N.Y. 10036
Controlling agency of musical comedies and light operas, including works by Rudolph Friml, Herbert Stothart, and others.

Music Theatre International. Catalog of Musical Plays. N.Y., 1973.
A catalog of all musicals controlled by the agency; gives complete credits, synopses, excerpts from reviews, awards, list of songs from the score, recording of cast album; and a list of the orchestrations available for all the plays.
Address: 119 West 57th St.
          New York, N.Y. 10019

Reinheimer & Cohen, 11 East 44th Street, New York, N.Y. 11232
Controlling agency for all Rodgers and Hammerstein shows and others including some Irving Berlin works.

Samuel French's Basic Catalog of Plays. N.Y., Samuel French.
Begun in 1830, the oldest of the four leading play agencies who control production rights to plays. Basic catalog revised periodically with additional annual supplements; it contains much reference material about each play which would be difficult to find elsewhere. Gives synopses of plays, type of casts required, source of plots, excerpts from reviews. Besides monologues, one-act plays, skits, stunts, and teaching material, the latest hits from Broadway, Off-Broadway, London and the rest of the world are included. Fees for royalties and scripts including unpublished plays in manuscript are included.
Address: 25 West 45th Street
          New York, N.Y. 10036
      and 7623 Sunset Blvd.
          Hollywood, Calif. 90046

Tams-Witmark, Music Library, Inc., New York. Complete Catalog
    of Broadway Musical Shows. 38th ed., 1974.
World's largest and most experienced company in supplying musicals

to amateur and professional groups since 1870. Issued annually, the catalog is kept up to date by the company's periodical <u>Musical Show</u>. Gives synopses, production scenes, casts of characters, excerpts from critics' reviews.
Address: 757 Third Avenue
           New York, N.Y.   10017

Theatre Maximus, 1650 Broadway, Suite 501, New York, N.Y. 10019
Controlling agency for popular musicals for stock and amateur productions; publishes bulletins and fliers as plays are released for publication.

FILMS

CHRONOLOGY OF STUDY GUIDES

1889-1930   Blum, Daniel. A Pictorial History of the
        Silent Screen. N.Y., Grosset & Dunlap,
        1853.
        A collection of over 3,000 stills and photo-
        graphs covering the silent film period, 1889-
        1930. A brief narrative accompanies the ar-
        rangement of films by years; title and name
        index.

1890-1950   Sadoul, Georges. French Film. London,
        Falcon Press, 1953.
        A survey of the cultural, economic and artistic
        influences of the French film, 1890-1950.
        Mostly a catalog of dates and achievements
        with stills.

1890-1970   Perry, George. The Great British Picture
        Show from the 90s to the 70s. N.Y.,
        Hill and Wang, 1974.
        A survey of British films with an index giving
        titles leading to criticism; includes a bio-
        graphical guide to British cinema giving credits.

1894-1912   Niver, Kemp R. Motion Pictures from the Li-
        brary of Congress Paper Print Collection,
        1894-1912. Berkeley, University of Calif.,
        1967.
        Catalog of 3,000 films provides dates, names
        of players, length and condition of films,
        synopsis of action.

1894-   U.S. Copyright Office. Motion Pictures, 1894-
        Wash., D.C., U.S. Gov't Print Off., 1951-
        60.
        Lists releasing agent, producer, director,
        author, series, etc. and date of copyright.
        Valuable source to determine release date in
        order to locate reviews of the source if based
        on another work. The Library of Congress
        Catalog--Motion Pictures & Filmstrips, pub-
        lished as part of the National Union Catalog
        keeps the series up to date.

1895-1928   Brownlow, Kevin. The Parade's Gone By.
                        N.Y., Knopf, 1968.
                   A survey of the silent film mainly through
                   interviews; exceptional collection of stills.
                   Covers the period 1895 through 1928.

1895-1969   Leprohon, Pierre. The Italian Cinema. Rev.
                        ed. N.Y., Praeger, 1972.
                   Detailed and thorough history of the Italian
                   cinema from its genesis in 1895 through 1969,
                   relating trends within the context of Italy's
                   cultural, political and social crisis; includes
                   biographical dictionary; stills.

1895-1969   Manvell, Roger, and Heinrich Fraenkel. The
                        German Cinema. N.Y., Praeger Publish-
                        ers, 1971.
                   A lucid account of the German cinema, 1895-
                   1969; includes interpretations of selected films
                   and detailed account of the propaganda film;
                   stills.

1895-1970   The British Film Institute Catalog, 1895-1970,
                        ed. by Denis Gifford. N.Y., McGraw-
                        Hill Book Co., 1973.
                   The first complete catalog of every British
                   film produced for public entertainment since
                   the invention of cinematography. Gives credits,
                   cast and a one-line annotation of each film.

1896-1929   Pratt, George C. Spellbound in Darkness; a
                        History of the Silent Film. Rev. ed.
                        Greenwich, Conn., New York Graphic So-
                        ciety, 1973.
                   A compilation of original readings from con-
                   temporary sources pertaining to films produced
                   and imported into the United States during the
                   major period of silent films, 1896-1929. Gives
                   synopses, casts, credits, commentaries of se-
                   lected films; stills.

1896-1929   Low, Rachel. The History of the British Film,
                        1896-1929. London, Allen and Unwin, c.
                        1948-1971. 4 vols.
                   Monumental work in process based upon re-
                   search of the History Committee of the British
                   Film Institute; contains much valuable reference
                   material plus contemporary criticism and synop-
                   ses of films.

1896-1971   Leyda, Jay. Dianying: an Account of Films
                        and the Film Audience in China. Cam-
                        bridge, Massachusetts Institute of Tech-

nology Press, 1972.
Survey of films from 1896-1971; includes a section of biographical material and stills.

1896-1971   Richie, Donald. <u>Japanese Cinema; Film Style</u>
<u>and National Character</u>. Garden City,
<u>Doubleday, 1971</u>.
Traces development of the Japanese cinema
from 1896-1971; stills.

1896-1973   Danish Film Institute. <u>Danish Films</u>. Køben-
havn, Udenrigsministeriets Presse og Kul-
turafdeling, 1973.
Brief survey of films 1896-1960, and for the
modern era 1960 to 1973; stills.

1897-1965   Richie, Donald. <u>The Japanese Movie; an Il-</u>
<u>lustrated History</u>. Tokyo, Kodansha In-
ternational; Rutland, Vt., Japan Publishers
Trading Co., 1966.
A survey of the Japanese film with illustrations.

1897-1969   Rangoonwalla, Firoze. <u>Indian Filmography;</u>
<u>Silent and Hindi Films, 1897-1969</u>. Bom-
bay, Bishwanath Das, J. Udeshi, 1970.
Development of Indian cinema with filmography
from the beginnings.

1898-1970   Skvorechy, Josef. <u>All the Bright Young Men</u>
<u>and Women; a Personal History of the</u>
<u>Czech Cinema</u>. Toronto, Peter P. Martin
Associates, 1971.
A history of Czech cinema for a film list
covering years 1898-1970; stills.

1900-1969   Schuster, Mel. <u>Motion Picture Performers:</u>
<u>a Bibliography of Magazine and Periodical</u>
<u>Articles, 1900-1969</u>. Metuchen, N.J.,
Scarecrow Press, 1971. Suppl., 1976.
A companion to the following; performers are
arranged alphabetically with citations listed
chronologically.

1900-1972   Schuster, Mel. <u>Motion Picture Directors: a</u>
<u>Bibliography of Magazine and Periodical</u>
<u>Articles, 1900-1972</u>. Metuchen, N.J.,
Scarecrow Press, 1973.
An alphabetical and chronological arrangement
of articles in English language devoted to directors, filmmakers and animators.

1905-1970   Cowie, Peter. <u>Sweden</u>. London, A. Zwemmer; N.Y., <u>A. S.</u> Barnes, 1970. 2 vols.

Contains survey of the cinema, c. 1905-1970,
giving biographical notes and filmographies of
directors, actors, actresses, writers, producers; gives plot synopses and credits; as-
sessment of the themes, trends; bibliography,
stills; title index of films.

1907-1971   Leyda, Jay. Kino, a History of the Russian
                    and Soviet Film. N.Y., Collier Books,
                    1973.
                 Documented history of the development of
                 films, 1907-1971; includes bibliography and
                 stills.

1908-1928   Weaver, John T., comp. Twenty Years of
                    Silents, 1908-1928. Metuchen, N.J.,
                    Scarecrow Press, 1971.
                 A guide to the screen credits of actors,
                 actresses, directors and producers of silent
                 films.

1908-1974   The British Film Institute. Film Title Index,
                    1908-1974. London, World Microfilms.
                 Contains details of over 200,000 films pro-
                 duced throughout the world since the inception
                 of the cinema; includes feature films, docu-
                 mentaries and cartoons, giving credits, synop-
                 ses and references to reviews and articles.
                 A two-yearly continuation service is planned
                 by the Institute, the most complete collection
                 on the cinema in the world.

1909-1957   Lauritzen, Einar. Swedish Films. N.Y.,
                    Museum of Modern Art Film Library, 1962.
                 Brief survey of films covering 1909-1957; in-
                 cludes biographical notes of directors; stills.

1915-1972   Nobile, Philip, ed. Favorite Movies: Critics'
                    Choice. N.Y., Macmillan, 1973.
                 A collection of critical articles, all especially
                 written in 1972, in retrospect, giving critical
                 views of favorite films from "Birth of a Na-
                 tion" (1915) to "A Clockwork Orange" (1972).

1917-1967   Pisarevskii, Dmitrii Sergeevich. 100 Soviet
                    Films. Sto Fil'mov Sovetskogo Kino.
                    Moskava, Iskusstvo, 1967.
                 An analysis of 100 key Russian films, 1917-
                 1967; gives critical commentaries; scene by
                 scene analysis; production information; stills;
                 text in Russian.

1915-1970   Film-TV Daily Yearbook of Motion Pictures.

N.Y., Film Daily, 1918-1970; Microfilm
ed.: N.Y., Arno, 1972.
A basic tool on film history. Discusses a
wide variety of subjects pertinent to the film
industry: labor problems, court decisions,
forecasts for the coming year, censorship
questions, use of films in education. Has
cumulative alphabetical list of approximately
33,000 films issued since 1915, together with
date of review in Film Daily (superseded by
Film and Television Daily).

1920-1955 Huaco, George A. The Sociology of Film Art.
    N.Y., Basic Books, 1965.
A documented study of film art: German expressionism (1920-1931); Soviet expressive re-
alism (1925-1930); Italian neorealism (1945-
1955).

1925-1939 London Film Society Programmes. N.Y.,
    Arno Press. Reprint ed., 1972.
Contains complete programmes of the Society
issued in connection with 108 sessions during
which approximately 900 features, 1925-1939,
were shown. Programs include notes about
directors, performers, scenarists with synopses and background material, credits, dates
and technical data; concise critiques of signifi-
cant films. New introduction by George Am-
berg and new cumulative index.

1925-1945 Balcon, Michael, and H. Forsyth Hardy, and
    others. Twenty-Four Years of British
    Films, 1925-1945. London, Falcon Press,
    1947.
Survey of British films for the period; includes both theatrical features and documentaries; stills.

1926-1935 Writers' Program, Work Projects Administra-
    tion, N.Y. The Film Index. Vol. 1:
    The Film as Art. N.Y., Museum of
    Modern Art Film Library and H. W. Wil-
    son Co., 1941.
A basic film bibliography for which only the
first volume was ever published. Covers history of the film 1926-1935. Useful, besides
basic reference, for locating film titles giving
synopses, release dates, national origin,
credits; detailed subject groupings.

1926-1944 Garcia Riera, Emilio. Historia Documental
    del Cine Mexicano. Mexico, Ediciones

Era, 1969-1970. 2 vols.
Documented study of Mexican cinema, 1929-
1944; gives plot synopses and critical analysis;
includes bibliography and illustrations. Text
in Spanish.

1927-1958   Blum, Daniel. A Pictorial History of the
                        Talkies. N.Y., Putnam, 1958.
                   A collection of stills and photographs with
                   brief narrative covers films from 1927 to
                   1958; index by film title and name.

1927-1963   Dimmitt, Richard Bertrand. A Title Guide to
                        the Talkies. Metuchen, N.J., Scarecrow
                        Press, 1967. 2 vols.
                   A comprehensive listing of 16,000 feature-
                   length films from October 1927 until December
                   1963.   Gives title of novel, play, poem, short
                   story or screen story which was used as a
                   basis for the film.   Gives release dates of
                   films; determines how many times a particular
                   work has been made into a motion picture.

1928-1969   Enser, A. G. S. Filmed Books and Plays.
                        London, Andre Deutsch, 1971.
                   A list of books and plays from which films
                   have been made, 1928-1969. It is useful for
                   determining year film was made, author, title
                   change, film producing company, book publish-
                   er.

1929-1969   Weaver, John T., comp. Forty Years of
                        Screen Credits, 1929-1969. Metuchen,
                        N.Y., Scarecrow Press, 1970. 2 vols.
                   A handy guide to motion picture players'
                   credits.

1929-1972   Liehn, Antonin J. Closely Watched Films:
                        the Czechoslovak Experience. N.Y., In-
                        ternational Arts and Sciences Press, 1974.
                   Survey of the Czechoslovak film by interviews
                   with the prominent filmmakers; filmography of
                   their works, 1929-1972; includes index of film
                   titles.

1930-1939   Trent, Paul. Those Fabulous Movie Years:
                        The Thirties. Barre, Mass., Barre Pub-
                        lishing Co., 1975.
                   Presents the turbulent 30s as a highwater mark
                   for the movies in 500 black and white and color
                   stills and text on leading films for the 10-year
                   period.

1930-1967   Fuente, Maria Isabel de la. Indice Bibliogra-
fico del Cine Mexicano. Mexico, Talleres
de "Editorial America," 1967-
Bibliographic cross reference index of Mexican
films, 1930-1967. Text in Spanish.

1930-1970   McCann, Richard Dyre, and Edward S. Perry.
New Film Index; a Bibliography of Maga-
zine Articles in English, 1930-1970. N.Y.,
Dutton, 1975.
An updating of Film Index, Vol. 1: The Film
as Art, following the same classified arrangement; continues coverage of the film through
1970.

1930-1971   Batty, Linda. Retrospective Index to Film
Periodicals, 1930-1971. N.Y., Bowker,
1975.
Indexes 14 film journals in their entirety,
plus film reviews and articles from Village
Voice. Sections include: Index of Reviews
of Individual Films; Index of Film Subjects;
and Index of Book Review Citations.

1942/43-   Annuaire du Spectacle: Théâtre, Cinéma,
Musique, Radio, Télévision. Paris,
Raoult, Vol. 1, 1942/43-
Annual directory of theatres, producers, di-
rectors, actors, etc. in France, Belgium,
French-speaking Switzerland.

1945-1966   Nemeskurty, Istvan. Word and Image; History
of the Hungarian Cinema. Budapest, Cor-
vina Press, 1968.
A history covering films, 1945-1966; filmography, bibliography, stills.

1946-1970   Armes, Roy. French Cinema Since 1946.
2nd ed. London, Zwemmer; Cranbury,
N.J., A. S. Barnes, 1970. 2 vols.
Surveys the French film since 1946 covering
major directors, style, tradition; includes
filmographies, bibliographies, stills.

1947-1967   Twenty Years of Polish Cinema; Film 1947-
1967, introduced by Stanislaw Grzelecki;
still selection and captions by Alicja Hel-
man; design by Leck Zahorski. Warsaw,
Art and Film Publishers, 1969.
Stills, captions, notes and filmography of films.

1949-1964   Dimmitt, Richard Bertrand. An Actor Guide
to the Talkies. Metuchen, N.J., Scare-

crow Press, 1967.   2 vols.
A comprehensive guide listing 8,000 feature-
length films from January 1949 until December
1964, giving credits and casts.   Indexes some
30,000 actors by name and roles played.

1952-1965   Rondi, Gian Luigi.   Italian Cinema Today,
                        1952-1965.   London, Dennis Dobson, 1966.
                   A survey of films from Italy for the period in
                   text and stills.

1967-   Catalogo del Cine Argentino.   Buenos Aires,
                        Fondo Nacional de las Artes, 1967-
                   Gives synopses in Spanish, French, and
                   English, of films produced in Argentina; gives
                   cast, credit, stills and reviews of films.   An-
                   nual.

1970-1974   Turan, Kenneth and Stephen F. Zito.   Sinema:
                        American Pornographic Films and the Peo-
                        ple Who Make Them.   N.Y., Praeger,
                        1974.
                   A survey of the pornographic film industry
                   since the beginning of hard core shows in
                   1970 to the present.   Includes interviews with
                   producers, directors, actors, and comments
                   about the films themselves; includes stills.
                   The index provides access to discussion of the
                   films by title.

1972-1973   American Film Institute.   Guide to College
                        Courses in Film and Television, ed. by
                        Michele Herling.   Washington, D.C.,
                        Acropolis Books, 1973.
                   A comprehensive survey of colleges and uni-
                   versities offering facilities in film and tele-
                   vision based on a 1972-73 American Film In-
                   stitute survey.   The schools are arranged
                   alphabetically by state.

REVIEW INDEXING SERVICES

1896-1964   Bibliographie der Deutschen Zeitschriftenliteratur. (IBZ, Abt. A) Leipzig, Dietrich; N.Y., Kraus, 1896-1964.
Wide coverage is useful for finding materials in American and English periodicals as well as in French, Italian, and other European publications. For motion picture criticism check under "Film." Combined with Internationale Bibliographie der Zeitschriftenliteratur.

1900-1943   Bibliographie der Rezensionen. (IBZ, Abt. C) Leipzig, Dietrich; N.Y., Kraus, 1900-1943.
Indexes reviews of books printed in some 3,000 German periodicals and about 2,000 periodicals in languages other than German. A very comprehensive list, especially for American and English research libraries, as it indexes many American and English sets not included in Book Review Digest. Supplements the above.

1900-   Readers' Guide to Periodical Literature. N.Y., H. W. Wilson Co., 1900-
Films began to be listed in the 1905-09 volume under "Moving Pictures."

1900-   Essay and General Literature Index. N.Y., H. W. Wilson, 1900-
Indexes essays and criticism collected from books. Check under "Moving Pictures--Reviews."

1907-   Humanities Index. N.Y., H. W. Wilson, Co., 1974- . Formerly International Index to Periodicals, 1907-1965. Became Social Sciences and Humanities Index, 1965-1973. Title split into two parts in 1974.
Monthly cumulations with annual permanent volumes. Indexes international films under "Moving Picture reviews--single works," "Musical Comedies, Revues--Criticism."

1907-   Social Sciences Index. N.Y., H. W. Wilson, 1974- . Formerly International Index to

Periodicals, 1907-1965.   Became Social
Sciences and Humanities Index, 1965-1973.
Title split into two parts in 1974.
Monthly cumulations with annual permanent
volumes.   Indexes international films under
"Moving Picture reviews--single works,"
"Musical Comedies, Revues--Criticism."

1911-1943   Bibliographie der Fremdsprachigen Zeitschriften-
literatur.   (IBZ, Abt. B) Leipzig, Dietrich;
N.Y., Kraus, 1911-1943.
Indexes about 1, 400 periodicals and general
works in the principal non-German languages.
For dramatic criticism check under "Drama."
Merged into Internationale Bibliographie der
Zeitschriftenliteratur.

1915-   Sadoul, Georges.   Dictionary of Films.   Berkeley, University of California Press, 1972.
A discussion of some 1, 200 films including
those from lesser known countries, major works
including silent films.   For each film is given
a fairly complete list of credits, the running
time or length, a summary of the plot and a
critical appreciation.

1915-1972   Baer, D. Richard, ed.   The Film Buff's Bible
of Motion Pictures, 1915-1972.   Hollywood,
Calif., Hollywood Film Archive, 1972.
A comprehensive summary of information and
critical appraisal of some 13, 000 motion pictures with entries of films through September
1972.   It includes silent films, short features,
movies made for television, and movies which
have never been shown on television.   It gives
year released, running time, critical ratings,
distributor and comments.

1921-1930   American Film Institute.   The American Film
Institute Catalog of Motion Pictures Pro-
duced in the United States, ed. by Kenneth
W. Munden.   N.Y., R. R. Bowker, 1971-
Vol. F2, pts. 1 & 2, contains feature films,
1921-1930.   Gives release date, length, credits,
cast and synopsis as well as subject of film.
Part 2 is an index by subject/credit of the
films.   Subsequent volumes to cover information on every film, feature, short or newsreel,
made in the U.S. since 1893 are projected
through 1976.

1929-   Art Index.   N.Y., H. W. Wilson Co., 1929-
Contains reviews of films not necessarily on

art and is a good source for all types of cur-
rent films. Check under "Moving Pictures,"
"Moving Pictures--criticism, plots," and
"Moving picture reviews."

1930-   Maltin, Leonard, ed. TV Movies. N.Y., A
                 Signet Book, New American Library, 1969-
                 Gives one-paragraph review of each of about
                 8,000 films which have been shown on tele-
                 vision; includes major credits. Each new edi-
                 tion is enlarged; 1975 edition is expanded to
                 include 10,000 films. The four-star rating
                 system is used. Gives production date, run-
                 ning time, director, national origin, and major
                 players.

1936-   Films. N.Y., National Catholic Office for
                 Motion Pictures, 1936-
                 A comprehensive review of the year in motion
                 pictures.

1941-   Facts on File. N.Y., Facts on File, 1941-
                 Weekly national and foreign news reference
                 service with cumulative index. Consult index
                 under "Motion Pictures--N.Y., releases" to
                 obtain very short synopses of films; gives
                 basic credits and opening date of the films.

1945-1974   Film Review, ed. by F. Maurice Speed.
                 London, Macdonald & Co.: N.Y., A. S.
                 Barnes Co., 1945/46-1973/74.
                 Contains reviews, stills, credits for releases
                 of the year.

1946-   Film Evaluation Guide. N.Y., Educational
                 Film Library Association, 1946-1964,
                 1968, 1972-
                 Gives national origin of films, running times,
                 synopses, subject areas, dates, distributors
                 and addresses.

1949-   Index to Religious Periodical Literature.
                 Chicago, American Theological Library As-
                 sociation, 1949-
                 An author and subject index to journals in re-
                 ligion and related areas. Film reviews covers
                 also films with other than religious themes.
                 Check citations under "Moving Pictures re-
                 views."

1949-   Screen World. N.Y., Biblo & Tannen. Vol.
                 1, 1949-
                 Yearbook of films, edited by Daniel Blum

through 1967, continued by John Willis.   Gives
credits, stills, biographical data of players,
obituaries.   A companion to Theatre World.

1956/1957-   Landers Film Reviews.   Los Angeles, Landers
                          Associates, 1956/57-
                    An informative guide to 16mm films; issued
                    nine times per year with cumulative index
                    every five years.

1957-   Guide to the Performing Arts, ed. by S. Yan-
                          cey Belknap.   Metuchen, N.J., Scarecrow
                          Press, 1957-
                    Annual index listing articles and illustrations
                    from periodicals on music, dance, theatre,
                    opera, films, television and recordings.   In-
                    cludes history and criticism, reviews, bio-
                    graphical citations.   Contains many entries not
                    covered by other indexes.

1958-   Scheuer, Steven H.   Movies on TV.   N.Y.,
                          Bantam Books, 1958-
                    Formerly TV Key Movie Guide.   Each new
                    edition has deleted reviews of some films in-
                    cluded in earlier editions.   It keeps number of
                    films to about 8,000.   Gives production date,
                    national origin, cast of major stars only.
                    Four-star rating system is used, but tends to
                    overrate films.

1962-   British Humanities Index.   London, The Library
                          Association.   1962-
                    Published quarterly with annual cumulations;
                    supersedes The Subject Index to Periodicals,
                    published 1915-1961.   For criticism and re-
                    views of films and filming check under "Cinema"
                    for world-wide coverage.

1964-   International Film Guide, ed. by Peter Cowie.
                          N.Y., A. S. Barnes Co., 1964-
                    Annual world survey with reports from some
                    50 film-producing nations; includes book re-
                    views, film reviews, film schools, film festi-
                    vals and vast amount of related reference in-
                    formation.   Films are reviewed and listed un-
                    der their original language title with English
                    translations where appropriate.

1965-   Internationale Bibliographie der Zeitschriften-
                          literatur.   Leipzig, Dietrich; N.Y., Kraus,
                          1965-
                    A subject index to world periodical literature
                    in German with cross references from English

and French forms.   More than 7,600 periodicals are consulted.   A combination of the
three above bibliographies.

1967/1968-   Film, 67/68-   N.Y., Simon and Schuster.
                      Annual anthology of the National Society of
                      Film Critics.   Contains reviews and articles
                      on a selective list of films released during the
                      year.   Represents the work of the leading
                      American film reviewers.

1790-   Times, London. Index to The Times. 1790-
         1966, 1970-
         For film reviews check under "Cinematography"
         from 1941 to 1962. Beginning in 1963 check
         under "Films."

1851-   The New York Times Index: a Book of Record.
         N.Y., The New York Times Co., 1851-
         In this master key to the news, check under
         "Motion pictures--Reviews"; before 1944 check
         under "Moving pictures" for reviews of specific
         productions. This is good to use for titles
         prior to 1913 when coverage also begins in
         The New York Times Film Reviews, and until
         cumulated volumes of that title are published.

1913-   The New York Times Film Reviews. N.Y.,
         New York Times, 1913-
         Basic five-volume set, 1913-1968, contains
         18,000 critiques as published in The New York
         Times in their entirety and arranged chrono-
         logically. Subsequent two-year volumes bring
         an additional 1,100 reviews per volume. Pro-
         vides ready reference to virtually any question
         about motion pictures. Fully indexed, gives
         casts and credits.

1958-   Wall Street Journal Index. N.Y., Dow Jones
         & Co., 1958-
         Annual cumulation is divided into two sections:
         corporate news and general news. Check gen-
         eral news section under "Movie industry."
         Titles of the films reviewed will appear in the
         title of the newspaper article.

1960-   Index to The Christian Science Monitor. Ann
         Arbor, Michigan, University Microfilms,
         1960-
         For reviews of films check under "Movies" and
         then under individual title of the film.

1969-   Alternative Press Index. Toronto, Radical Re-

search Centre, 1969-
An index published quarterly to alternative and
underground publications "which amplify the cry
for social change and social justice." Check
under "Film Reviews," then alphabetical by
title of film for good coverage of the off-beat,
experimental, underground films as well as the
general type films.

1969-

National Observer Index.   Princeton, N.J.,
    Dow Jones & Co., 1969-
Annual cumulation of the newspaper articles
gives a one-sentence guide to the specific subject of the articles; thus for film reviews,
check under "Movies," and if the article is
about a specific film the title will be in the
annotation of the article.

1972-

Newspaper Index: Chicago Tribune; Los
    Angeles Times; New Orleans Times;
    Picayune; Washington Post.   Wooster,
    Ohio, Bell & Howell, Micro Photo Divi-
    sion, June 1972-
A combined index of the four named newspapers.   Check under "Motion Pictures--Re-
views."

CINEMA CRITICISM CHECKLISTS

1909-1939   Lounsbury, Myron Osborn. The Origins
of American Film Criticism, 1909-1939.
University of Pennsylvania doctoral dissertation. N.Y., Arno Press, 1973.
This work concentrates upon the literature
found in periodicals and books written for the
film-goer who seeks an appraisal of current
films or aesthetic trends. For this reason
fan magazines and trade journals have been
given only scant attention.

1927-1964   Salem, James M. A Guide to Critical Reviews. Metuchen, N.J., Scarecrow Press,
1966-1973. 4 pts. in 5 vols.
Part IV: The Screenplay, from "The Jazz Sing-
er" (1927) to "Dr. Strangelove" (1964); a two-
volume bibliography of critical reviews of
12, 000 American and foreign feature-length
screenplays; includes cross references to title
changes.

1930-1972   Bowles, Stephen E., comp. Index to Critical
Film Reviews in British and American
Film Periodicals: 1930-1972. N.Y.,
Burt Franklin, 1974. 2 vols.
A comprehensive listing of over 20, 000 reviews
of films, followed by a shorter listing of some
6, 000 reviews of books about films; also included are documentaries and shorts reviewed
during the period covered.

1944/45-   International Motion Picture Almanac. N.Y.,
Quigley Publications, 1944/45-
Lists feature releases cumulatively, giving
pertinent data and other information about the
motion picture industry.

1946-1973   Gerlach, John C., and Lana Gerlach. The
Critical Index. N.Y., Teachers College
Press, Columbia University, 1974.
A bibliography of articles on film in English,
1946-1973, arranged by names and topics; a

guide to articles about directors, producers,
actors, critics, screenwriters, cinematographers, specific films.

1972-   International Index to Film Periodicals.   N.Y.,
                    Bowker, 1972-
                 Indexes 59 film periodicals from 21 countries;
                 includes articles, reviews, essays, interviews,
                 and filmographies; issued annually.

1973-   Film Literature Index.   Albany, N.Y., Filmdex.
                    Vol. 1, 1973-
                 A quarterly subject, author index to interna-
                 tional film literature appearing in periodicals.
                 Most comprehensive survey available of the en-
                 tire spectrum of current periodical writing on
                 film.   Reviews of films are found with critical
                 and analytical articles under the title of the
                 film.

1974-   Hochman, Stanley, comp. & ed., A Library of
                    Film Criticism: American Film Directors.
                    N.Y., Frederick Ungar Pub. Co., 1974.
                 First volume in a projected series, this ar-
                 ranges alphabetically and chronologically under
                 each director's name, excerpts drawn from
                 specialized periodicals, general publications,
                 collections of film criticism, private clipping
                 files, and books on individual directors.
                 Sizable excerpts from critical evaluations of
                 films are given on 65 American film directors.
                 Contains index of critics and film titles.

1975-   Film Review Digest.   Millwood, N.Y., Kraus-
                    Thomson Organization, Ltd.   1975-
                 Digest of film reviews in alphabetical order
                 from two dozen newspapers and journals repre-
                 senting points of view from the United States,
                 Canada, and England.   Issued quarterly with
                 an annual cumulation.

COLLECTED REVIEWS OF INDIVIDUAL CRITICS

1895-1960   Altshuler, Thelma and Richard Paul Janaro.
          Responses to Drama; an Introduction to
          Plays and Movies. N.Y., Houghton Mifflin,
          1967.
          The purpose of this book is to assist playgoers
(or readers) and film viewers in making evaluations; in so doing, choice excerpts are given
from reviews, opinions on criticism by critics,
craft of the theatre and film, and a chronology
of theatre and film from the Age of Pericles
(5th Century) to Fellini's "La Dolce Vita" (1960).

1895-1967   Cowie, Peter. Seventy Years of Cinema.
          Cranbury, N.J., A. S. Barnes Co., 1969.
          Traces the history and development of the
movies by years, 1895-1967, with an index by
title of films reviewed. Illustrated with stills.

1895-1970   Wright, Basil. The Long View. N.Y., Knopf,
          1974.
          A collection of film reminiscences, essays,
criticism, covering the entire scope of films
from 1895-1970.

1896-1941   Kauffmann, Stanley, ed. American Film
          Criticism. N.Y., Liveright, 1972.
          Reviews of significant films at the time they
first appeared, from the beginning (Edison,
1896) to "Citizen Kane" (1941).

1896-1973   Lawton, Richard. A World of Movies; Seventy
          Years of Film History. N.Y., Delacorte
          Press, 1974.
          A concise history of the best world films
covered by excellent reproductions of unusual
stills from "The Kiss" (1896) to "The Last
Tango in Paris" (1973).

1902-1966   Renan, Sheldon. An Introduction to the Ameri-
          can Underground Film. N.Y., Dutton,
          1967.
          History and criticism of the avant-garde, ex-

perimental and underground film movement in
America; provides detailed accounts from the
beginning of careers and films of the most
prominent film-makers of this genre; gives
specific data on each title; includes an appendix
of film titles mentioned in the text giving descriptions of the films and distribution for rent
or sale.

1903-1971   Franklin, Joe. Classics of the Silent Screen;
a Pictorial Treasury. N.Y., Citadel
Press, 1959.
A history of the silent movies as seen through
50 selected films from "The Great Train Rob-
bery" (1903) to "Tabu" (1931) and an analysis
of 75 stars.

1905-1971   Bogle, Donald. Toms, Coons, Mulattoes, Mam-
mies, and Bucks; an Interpretive History
of Blacks in American Films. N.Y.,
Viking Press, 1973.
Surveys the role of blacks in American films
from "Wooing and Wedding a Coon" (1905) to
"Shaft" (1971).

1915-1936   Cooke, Alistair, ed. Garbo and the Night
Watchman. N.Y., McGraw-Hill, 1971.
Writings on films by British and American
critics which originally appeared in periodicals
in 1937, but which criticize films from "Birth
of a Nation" (1915) to "Camille" (1939); includes annotated index which gives date and di-
rector of films discussed; stills.

1915-1967   Crowther, Bosley. The Great Films; Fifty
Golden Years of Motion Pictures. N.Y.,
G. P. Putnam's Sons, 1967.
Critical analysis of films ranging from "The
Birth of a Nation" (1915) to "Ulysses" (1967).
Contains lengthy articles including credits; il-
lustrated with stills. Includes supplemental
list of 100 distinguished films.

1915-1967   Baxter, John. Sixty Years of Hollywood.
Cranbury, N.J., A. S. Barnes, 1973.
A year-by-year summary of American films
from "Birth of a Nation" (1915) to "Easy
Rider" (1969); contains selected reviews, il-
lustrated with stills.

1915-1969   Tyler, Parker. Underground Film; a Critical
History. N.Y., Grove Press, 1969.
Critical reviews of films covering the period

1915-1969, indicating the passage from avant-
garde to underground films. Filmography lists
individual film titles grouped by years.

1915-1970   Kinder, Marsha, and Beverley Houston. Close-
                       Up: a Critical Perspective on Films.
                       N.Y., Harcourt, 1972.
                   Examines in depth films which are accepted
                   examples of the aesthetic films from "Birth of
                   a Nation" (1915) to documentary, ethnic, war,
                   neo-realism, myth and politics in film, the
                   New French Wave, to "The Conformist" (1970).

1916-1970   Solomon, Stanley J., comp. The Classic
                       Cinema; Essays in Criticism. N.Y., Har-
                       court Brace Jovanovich, 1973.
                   Fourteen classic films are given in-depth study
                   by various critics, from "Intolerance" (1916)
                   to "Satyricon" (1970).

1919-1961   Tyler, Parker. Classics of the Foreign Film,
                       a Pictorial Treasury. N.Y., Citadel
                       Press, 1962.
                   A critical survey of the classic foreign film
                   from "The Cabinet of Dr. Caligari" (1919) to
                   "La Notte" (1961).

1920-1930   Macdonald, Dwight. Dwight Macdonald on
                       Movies. Englewood Cliffs, N.J., Prentice-
                       Hall, 1969.
                   Essays and reviews from his 40-year career
                   as a film commentator. Mainly on films of
                   the 1920s and 1930s; he has edited and an-
                   notated the reviews from the point of view of
                   1969.

1920-1948   Agate, James. Around Cinemas. Series 1 &
                       2. N.Y., Arno Press, 1946, 1948.
                   A selection of over 300 film reviews.

1920-1970   Clair, René. Cinema Yesterday and Today.
                       N.Y., Dover Publishers, 1972.
                   A mixture of personal memories with critical
                   perception and aesthetics in a survey of his en-
                   tire career and the whole of the film history;
                   a 50-year record of his work and cinema criti-
                   cism, 1920-1970.

1923-1959   Talbot, Daniel, ed. Film: an Anthology.
                       N.Y., Simon & Schuster, 1959.
                   Dating back to 1923, the articles are grouped
                   by aesthetics, social commentary, analysis, the-
                   ory and technique, and history.

1926-1970   Bayer, William. The Great Movies. N.Y.,
                        Grosset & Dunlap, 1973.
                   A critical analysis ranging from "Metropolis"
                   (1926) to "M*A*S*H" (1970); includes credits,
                   full index and outstanding color and black and
                   white photography reproductions.

1927-1965   MacCann, Richard Dyer, ed. Film: a
                        Montage of Theories. N.Y., Dutton, 1966.
                   A collection of 39 articles by leading film-
                   makers, critics and theoreticians, such as
                   Pudovkin, Eisenstein, René Clair, Hitchcock,
                   Vachel Lindsay, Parker Tyler, Ingmar Berg-
                   man, Carl Dreyer, Fellini, Mack Sennett and
                   others.

1928-1958   Rotha, Paul. Rotha on Film. N.Y., Fair
                        Lawn, Essential Books, 1958.
                   Sixty-odd brief reviews, articles, and cri-
                   tiques which appeared in a number of periodi-
                   cals and newspapers, beginning 1928.

1929-1970   Weinberg, Herman G. Saint Cinema. 2nd
                        ed. N.Y., Dover Pub., 1973.
                   Articles written during 1929-1970, dealing al-
                   most exclusively with the art film and the
                   serious artists.

1930-1939   Griffith, Richard. The Talkies; Articles and
                        Illustrations from Photoplay Magazine,
                        1928-1940. N.Y., Dover Pub., 1971.
                   A collection of 150 articles from Photoplay
                   which reveal the exaggerated and mythical fan
                   magazine writing of the 30s, but valuable as
                   history, reference, and comparison of other
                   types of reviews.

1930-1949   Zinman, David H. 50 Classic Motion Pictures;
                        the Stuff That Dreams Are Made Of. N.Y.,
                        Crown, 1970.
                   A survey of 50 films of the 1930s and 1940s
                   which the author considers distinguished, unique
                   or hilarious. Gives synopses, credits, cri-
                   tique, stills, with a good bibliography and in-
                   dex.

1930-1970   Boyum, Joy Gould, and Adrienne Scott. Film
                        as Film: Critical Responses to Film Art.
                        Boston, Allyn and Bacon, 1971.
                   Contains nearly 100 critical reviews on 25
                   modern classic films.

1934-1940   Greene, Graham. The Pleasure Dome. Lon-

don, Secker & Warburg, 1972.
Collected film criticism as published in the
Spectator and Night and Day, covers some 400
films, 1934-1940.   American edition published
as Graham Greene on Film, N.Y., Simon
& Schuster, 1972.   Illustrated with stills.

1934-1942   Ferguson, Otis.   Film Criticism.   Philadel-
                     phia, Temple University Press, 1971.
                 A collection of his articles originally written
                 for the New Republic, 1934-1942.   A valuable
                 view of Hollywood before the advent of tele-
                 vision.

1935-1938   Van Doren, Mark.   The Private Reader.   N.Y.,
                     Henry Holt, 1942; Kraus, 1968.
                 Selected articles and reviews; the section on
                 movies includes reviews for those made 1935-
                 1938.

1937-1943   Villaurrutia, Xavier.   Critica Cinematografica.
                     Mexico, Direccion General de Difusion Cul-
                     tural, 1970.
                 Critical film reviews, 1937-1943.   Text in
                 Spanish.

1941-1948   Agee, James.   Agee on Film, Vol. 1: Re-
                     views and Comments.   N.Y., McDowell,
                     Obolensky, 1958.
                 A collection of his reviews written for The
                 Nation and Time, 1941-1948.

1941-1970s   Murray, Edward.   Nine American Film Critics;
                     a Study of Theory and Practice.   N.Y.,
                     Frederick Ungar, 1975.
                 A critical appraisal of the work of leading
                 critics: James Agee, Robert Warshow, Andrew
                 Sarris, Parker Tyler, John Simon, Pauline
                 Kael, Stanley Kauffmann, Vernon Young, and
                 Dwight Macdonald; a guide to current critical
                 standards and performance, and a comparison
                 of critical responses to such movements as
                 Italian Neo-Realism and the French New Wave.

1945-1958   Bazin, Andre.   What Is Cinema?   Berkeley,
                     University of California Press, 1967-1971.
                     4 vols.
                 Classic essays of film criticism translated
                 from the French by Hugh Gray.

1945-1967   Sarris, Andrew, ed.   The Film.   Indianapolis,
                     Bobbs Merrill, 1968.
                 A collection of selected film reviews by Kael,

Archer, Alpert, Bresson, Croce, Simon and
others mostly from Film Culture, N.Y. Times
Magazine, Sight and Sound, Canadian Art, National Review, Village Voice, and The New
Leader.

1945-1974   Mellen, Joan. Voices from the Japanese
                      Cinema. N.Y., Liveright, 1975.
An inside view of Japanese films, directors,
performers; provides new insights of the film
"renaissance" in Japan; includes interviews
with directors and discussions of films.

1946-1971   Farber, Manny. Negative Space. N.Y.,
                      Praeger, 1971; reissued under title Movies,
                      N.Y., Stonehill, 1974.
His essays and reviews on films from approximately 1946 to 1971.

1950-1959   Dowdy, Andrew. "Movies Are Better Than
                      Ever"; Wide-Screen Memories of the
                      Fifties. N.Y., William Morrow, 1973.
Film reviews and criticism for the 1950s when
screens became giants.

1950-1959   Duprey, Richard A. Just Off the Aisle; the
                      Ramblings of a Catholic Critic. West-
                      minster, Maryland, The Newman Press,
                      1962.
Criticism of plays and films from a Catholic
viewpoint; articles appeared in The Critic, The
Catholic World, and The Catholic Standard and
Times, mostly during the 1950s.

1952-1972   Young, Vernon. On Film: Unpopular Essays
                      on a Popular Art. N.Y., Quadrangle
                      Books, 1972.
Lengthy reviews of films which include ob-
scure and short films also, as published in the
Hudson Review, and other periodicals approximately from 1952 to 1972.

1955-1969   Sarris, Andrew. Confessions of a Cultist:
                      On the Cinema, 1955-1969. N.Y., Simon
                      & Schuster, 1970.
Film reviews from Film Culture and The Village
Voice.

1956-1971   Sitney, P. Adams, ed. Film Culture Reader.
                      N.Y., Praeger, 1971.
Anthology of articles from Film Culture containing critical analysis of the avant-garde film

in America during the period 1956-1971.
Covers auteur theory, cinema of structure,
cosmic cinema; traces the development of the
American underground and noncommercial
cinema and the history of film as an original
art form.

1957-1967   Tynan, Kenneth. Tynan Right & Left: Plays,
                       Films, People, Places and Events. N.Y.,
                       Atheneum, 1967.
                   Critical pieces written from 1957 to 1967 of
                   plays and films including other performing
                   arts, public spectacles and events, places and
                   people. Check index for titles of plays and
                   films criticized.

1958-1965   Kael, Pauline. I Lost It at the Movies. Bos-
                       ton, Little, Brown, 1965.
                   Reviews and critical essays of films for the
                   late '50s and '60s as originally published in
                   Atlantic Monthly, Film Quarterly, Partisan
                   Review, Sight and Sound, Massachusetts Re-
                   view, Kulchur, Art Film Publications, Second
                   Coming, Film Culture, and Moviegoer.

1958-1965   Kauffmann, Stanley. A World on Film: Criti-
                       cism and Comment. N.Y., Harper &
                       Row, 1966.
                   His critical essays and reviews on films from
                   The New Republic, 1958-1965.

1959-1971   Mekas, Jonas. Movie Journal: The Rise of
                       the New American Cinema, 1959-1971.
                       N.Y., Macmillan, 1972.
                   A collection of articles on films as published
                   in The Village Voice, 1959-1971, but covering
                   many films of earlier periods. The index
                   gives titles of all films discussed regardless
                   of publication date of the articles.

1960-1971   Pechter, William S. Twenty-four Times a
                       Second. N.Y., Harper and Row, 1971.
                   Analysis of films, 1960-1971, as originally
                   published in Commentary, Commonweal, Ken-
                   yon Review, Moviegoer, Sight and Sound, Lon-
                   don Magazine, Contact, Tulane Drama Review,
                   Film Quarterly and Film Comment.

1960-1971   Gilliatt, Penelope. Unholy Fools; Wits,
                       Comics, Disturbers of the Peace: Film
                       & Theater. N.Y., Viking Press, 1973.
                   A collection of writings on films and the thea-
                   tre which originally appeared in The Guardian,

Harpers/Queen, The New Yorker, The Observer, Spectator, and Vogue, 1960-1971.

1960-1971   McCrindle, Joseph F., comp. Behind the
                   Scenes; Theater and Film Interviews from
                   the Transatlantic Review. N.Y., Holt,
                   Rinehart & Winston, 1971.
                   Discussion on contemporary theater and films
                   with Inge, Quintero, Marcel Marceau, Tony
                   Richardson, Gore Vidal, Jules Feiffer, Ed-
                   ward Albee, Joan Littlewood, Federico Fel-
                   lini, Alan Schneider, and others. These
                   articles originally appeared in the Transatlantic
                   Review, London, in 60s and early 70s.

1960-1971   Eberhard, Wolfram. The Chinese Silver
                   Screen. Taipei, Formosa, The Orient
                   Cultural Service, 1972.
                   Abstracts of 329 Hong Kong and Taiwanese mo-
                   tion pictures shown between 1960 and 1971;
                   gives synopses and comments about the films
                   and audience reaction; place and date shown,
                   but no credits are given.

1960-1973   Sarris, Andrew. The Primal Screen; Essays
                   on Film and Related Subjects. N.Y.,
                   Simon & Schuster, 1973.
                   A collection of articles of the '60s and '70s
                   which appeared in Film Culture, New York
                   Times, Mid-Century, and Village Voice.

1963-1966   Battcock, Gregory. The New American Cine-
                   ma; a Critical Anthology. N.Y., Dutton,
                   1967.
                   Focus on underground, independent, radical,
                   expanded cinema in survey, theory and criti-
                   cism in 29 articles by the filmmakers and the
                   artists involved; from articles published in The
                   Nation, Film Culture, Hudson Review and others.

1963-1966   Simon, John. Private Screenings. N.Y.,
                   Macmillan, 1967.
                   Film reviews which appeared in The New Lead-
                   er, 1963-1966.

1963-1967   Crist, Judith. The Private Eye, the Cowboy,
                   and the Very Naked Girl; Movies from Cleo
                   to Clyde. Chicago, Holt, Rinehart & Win-
                   ston, 1968.
                   Reviews of films from "Cleopatra" (1963) to
                   "Bonnie and Clyde" (1967) as originally pub-
                   lished in New York Herald Tribune, World
                   Journal Tribune, Vogue, Journal of the Pro-

ducers Guild of America.

1965-1968   Kael, Pauline. <u>Kiss Kiss Bang Bang</u>. Boston,
Little, Brown, 1968.
Critical essays and 180 capsule reviews of
films, 1965-1968, continued as in her previous
collection.

1965-1971   Schickel, Richard. <u>Second Sight</u>. N.Y.,
Simon & Schuster, 1972.
Reviews originally published in <u>Life</u>, from
"Darling" (1965) to "Gimme Shelter" (1971).

1966-1970   Kauffmann, Stanley. <u>Figures of Light: Film
Criticism and Comment</u>. N.Y., Harper
& Row, 1971.
His critical essays and reviews mainly from
<u>The New Republic</u> and <u>New American Review</u>,
1966-1970.

1966-1971   Wall, James M. <u>Church and Cinema; a Way
of Viewing Film</u>. Grand Rapids, Mich.,
Eerdmans, 1971.
Contains reviews from <u>The Christian Advocate</u>,
1966-1971, in which a pastor speaks for a new
and enlightened understanding between church
and cinema.

1967-1970   Simon, John. <u>Movies into Film</u>. N.Y., Dial
Press, 1971.
His film criticism from <u>The New Leader</u>, 1967-
1970.

1968-1969   Adler, Renata. <u>A Year in the Dark: Journal
of a Film Critic, 1968-69</u>. N.Y., Random
House, 1969.
A collection of 130 of her film reviews which
appeared in <u>The New York Times</u>.

1968-1969   Kael, Pauline. <u>Going Steady</u>. Boston, Little,
Brown, 1970.
Movie reviews which originally appeared in <u>The
New Yorker</u>, 1968-1969.

1968-1970   Reed, Rex. <u>Big Screen, Little Screen</u>. N.Y.,
Macmillan, 1971.
Collected TV and film reviews, 1968-1970, as
published in Esquire, Queen, Cosmopolitan,
<u>New York Times, New York Magazine of the
Herald Tribune, Playbill, Playboy, Woman's
Wear Daily, Status, This Week, Eye</u>, and
<u>Holiday</u>. His collections of interviews and es-
says: <u>Do You Sleep in the Nude?</u> <u>Conversa</u>-

tions in the Raw, and People Are Crazy Here, will augment the usefulness of the critical reviews.

1969-1972 Kael, Pauline. Deeper into Movies. Boston, Little, Brown, 1973.
Film reviews which appeared in The New Yorker, September 1969 through March 1972.

1970-1974 Kauffmann, Stanley. Living Images. N.Y., Harper & Row, 1975.
A collection of his film reviews 1970-1974 as they originally appeared in The New Republic, Performance, and Horizon. Contains a combined alphabetical listing of all films reviewed in his previous books.

LEADING FILM PERIODICALS

1905-
Variety. N.Y., Variety, Inc. 1905-
Weekly since 1905, an over-all review coverage
of films, television, radio, stage, music, records, literati, vaudenitery. The Music Index
is its only indexing source.

1907-
Motion Picture Herald. N.Y., Quigley Pub.
    Co., 1907-
Issued bi-weekly, a trade journal directed to
motion picture owners; gives brief descriptive
reviews, and general business news from the
world of producers, distributors, and exhibi-
tors; includes longer in-depth articles and the
"Release Chart and Review Index."

1925-
The New Yorker. N.Y., New Yorker Maga-
    zine, Vol. 1, 1925-
General sophisticated magazine; the film reviews are among the best available. Check
current weekly issues for criticism and for
older issues consult Music Index and Readers'
Guide to Periodical Literature where it is indexed.

1927-1933
Close-Up, a Magazine Devoted to the Art of the
    Film. London, Pool. Vol. 1-10, 1927-
    1933.
One of the first journals devoted to serious
film criticism. Vol. 10 includes indexes by
subject and film title.

1927-1934
Hound and Horn. Portland, Me., Hound &
    Horn, Inc., 1927-1934.
Little magazine of the avant-garde in literature
and all the arts, including the movies.

1932-
Sight and Sound. London, British Film Insti-
    tute, 1932-
Outstanding for film reviews and criticism.

1934-
Monthly Film Bulletin. London, British Film
    Institute, 1934-

Reviews some 60 to 75 films per issue, descriptive and critical in nature; similar to Filmfacts.

1935-   Catholic Film Newsletter. N.Y., Division for
                     Film and Broadcasting of the U.S. Catholic
                     Conference, 1935-
                 Critical reviews on the moral and aesthetic aspects of movies; beginning with volume 34, Jan. 15, 1969, a more comprehensive review service was started; newsletter is published twice per month with an annual index and a supplemental index rating sheet issued every 6 to 8 weeks.

1935-   Cue. N.Y., Cue Publishing Co., 1935-
                 Weekly guide to New York City with good coverage of reviews of theatre, movies, and television.

1937-   Bianco e Nero. Rome, Ernesto G. Laura,
                     1937-
                 A leading Italian journal which publishes reviews, articles, interviews, and filmographies.

1945-   Film Quarterly. Berkeley, University of California Press, 1958- . Formerly Hollywood Quarterly, 1945-51; Quarterly of Film, Radio & Television, 1952-57.
                 Lengthy reviews of films as well as reviews of books about films; issues annual index. More scholarly reviews than some others. The definitive reviews stress analysis rather than opinion. There are also short notices covering experimental, documentary and other films not in theatrical release and thus not commented upon by the weekly film reviewers.

1951-   Films in Review. N.Y., National Board of Review of Motion Pictures. Vol. 1, 1950-
                 Issued bi-monthly; contains film reviews, stills, book reviews, and biographical career articles on players and directors; issues cumulative indexes.

1951-   Cahiers du Cinéma. Paris, Les Editions de
                     l'Etoile, 1951-
                 Consists mainly of film criticism, interviews with film directors, historical and theoretical articles about films with a political slant; published in both French and English editions.

1952-   Positif; Revue Périodique de Cinéma. Paris,

Editions le Terrain Vague, 1952-
A balanced report of French cinema in particular and world cinema in general containing
some of the best film critics in Europe; also
includes interviews, articles on film-makers
and films, and regular reviews of current
films; a companion to Cahiers du Cinéma.

1954- Films and Filming. London, Hansom Books,
       Vol. 1, 1954-
       Contains book reviews, film reviews, stills;
       a companion to Plays and Players; issued
       monthly.

1955- Film Culture. N.Y., Jonas Mekas, 1955-
       Includes articles, reviews, interviews; slanted
       toward the experimental and underground film;
       includes festivals and critical notes.

1957- Soviet Film. Moscow, Kalashny Pereulok,
       1957-
       Covers the current Soviet films, with his-
       torical articles, interviews, documentary and
       feature films.

1958- Film Facts. N.Y., American Film Institute.
       Vol. 1, 1958-
       Issued semi-monthly; gives credits and digests
       of film reviews from periodicals. Covers six-
       teen nationwide reviews. Issues frequent in-
       dexes throughout the year with an annual cumu-
       lation.

1958- New Leader; a Bi-weekly of News and Opinion.
       N.Y., American Labor Conference on In-
       ternational Affairs, 1958-
       Contains longer than average reviews of films.
       Check the subject index of each volume under
       "Movies."

1959- Chaplin: Tidskrift foer Film. Stockholm,
       Sweden, Svenska Filminstitute, 1959-
       A Scandinavian film magazine which has been
       called "a touchstone for accuracy and often a
       forum for polemical debate," issued nine times
       per year; contains film reviews, stills, inter-
       views with directors and technicians; current
       international news stories on films.

1961- L'Avant-Scène du Cinéma. Paris, No. 1,
       1961-
       Film reviews and complete filmscripts are in-
       cluded in each issue; contains stills, bio-

graphical information, with an international
coverage of films.

1962-   Film Comment. Brookline, Mass., Film
         Comment Pub. Co., 1962-
         Scholarly articles of filmography, underground
         films, anthropological films, and interviews
         with directors.

1962-   Los Angeles Times Calendar. Los Angeles
         Times.
         Weekly magazine included in the Sunday edition
         of the Los Angeles Times, began as a separate
         magazine in 1962; covers events with particu-
         larly good reviews and criticism of films,
         plays, music, and art. Check weekly issues
         for new openings and also short synopsis of
         current titles playing. For back issues check
         Newspaper Index.

1965-   Film Society Review. N.Y., American Federa-
         tion of Film Societies, 1965-
         Issued monthly, includes overviews of televi-
         sion, international film, feature articles on
         directors, films, and history of the cinema.

1966-   Take One. Montreal, Peter Lebensold, 1966-
         Bi-monthly of international articles about films
         and major directors who "have something to
         say."

1967-   Cineaste, N.Y., Cineaste Magazine, 1967-
         Quarterly of film, magazine, and book re-
         views, and special reports engaged in the
         movement of social change, featuring material
         on political films and film makers.

1968-   Silent Picture. London, Anthony Slide; Cin-
         cinnati, First Media Press, 1968-
         A quarterly publication containing articles ex-
         clusively on the study of the silent film; film-
         ographies, film reviews, biographies, inter-
         views, stills.

1969-   Views and Reviews Magazine. Milwaukee, Wis.,
         Views and Reviews Productions, 1969-
         Quarterly publication containing film, book,
         and record reviews, with articles and statistics
         about the motion picture industry.

1970-   New Cinema Review. N.Y., 1970-
         Almost entirely devoted to reviews and inter-
         views with members of the underground, avant-
         garde film.

1971-   The Film Journal.   Hollins, Va., Vol. 1,
                    1971-
                 Contains new source material and documents
                 about significant films of all types, contem-
                 porary and historical, American and foreign;
                 gives scholarly appraisals from a wide variety
                 of disciplines and viewpoints, filmographies,
                 biographies, bibliographies and other pertinent
                 information about film sources and publications.

1972-   The Journal of the Popular Film.   Ohio, Bowl-
                    ing Green University Press, Vol. 1, 1972-
                 Quarterly publication contains articles on film
                 theory and criticism, interviews, filmography,
                 etc.

1972-   Film Index.   Mosman Bay, Australia, John
                    Howard Reid, No. 1, 1972-
                 Articles include interviews, book and film re-
                 views, stills, and a companion continuing bi-
                 ographical directory in alphabetical form.   Is-
                 sued monthly.

1975-   The Revue Internationale d'Histoire du Cinéma.
                    Paris, l'Avant-Scène; Iowa City, William
                    Gilcher, 1975-
                 A quarterly publication issued on six micro-
                 fiches in black and white and color, each on a
                 given subject, study or document always ac-
                 companied by a critical analysis.

DOCUMENTARY AND FACTUAL FILMS

1895-1973   Barnouw, Erik. Documentary: a History of
the Non-Fiction Film. N.Y., Oxford University Press, 1974.
An international survey of over 700 documentary
films of diverse periods and places; covers the
full range of film history from 1895 through
1973; includes stills; titles of the films discussed with production dates are included in
the index.

1908-1970s   MacCann, Richard Dyer. The People's Films:
a Political History of U.S. Government Mo-
tion Pictures. N.Y., Hastings House, 1973.
A basic history of the federal government use
of films from 1908 to 1945. Originally the author's Ph.D. dissertation at Harvard University,
new material has been added with coverage to
the '70s.

1916-1972   Index to 16mm Educational Films. Los Angeles, National Information Center for Educational Media, University of Southern
California. 4th ed., 1973. 3 vols.
Gives synopsis, running time, date, subjects,
audience appeal for approximately 70,000 titles;
includes a directory of producers and distributors.

1920-1970   Barsam, Richard Meran. Nonfiction Film: a
Critical History. N.Y., Dutton, 1973.
A survey covering documentary and factual
films with emphasis on American and British
productions from 1920 through 1970; includes
discussions of the producers, directors, camera
techniques, titles and plot explications.

1922-1951   Starr, Cecile, ed. Ideas on Film. N.Y.,
Funk & Wagnalls Co., 1951.
A collection of articles and film reviews as
originally published in Saturday Review of
Literature and Film Forum Review, 1946 to
1951. The films selected are designed essen-

tially to influence what people think. Many of
the reviews are of older films reviewed as
classics at a later date of re-release.

1922-1970   Jacobs, Lewis. The Documentary Tradition.
                       N.Y., Hopkinson & Blake, 1971.
                   An illustrated survey of the documentary film
                   from "Nanook of the North" (1922) to "Wood-
                   stock" (1970).

1922-1970   Levin, G. Roy. Documentary Explorations.
                       N.Y., Doubleday, 1972.
                   Covers the history of the documentary film
                   through 15 interviews with film makers; con-
                   tains brief outline of history of the documentary
                   film including coverage of key titles.

1922-1971   Parlato, Salvatore J., Jr. Films--Too Good
                       for Words. N.Y., Bowker, 1972.
                   A directory of nearly 1,000 nonnarrated 16mm
                   films; educational films that communicate pic-
                   torially rather than having a narration, relying
                   to convey the message by picture and sound
                   rather than with words. Includes classic si-
                   lent films as well as modern films; gives sy-
                   nopses and other information; title index, sub-
                   ject index, and distributor list.

1926-1945   Arts Enquiry. The Factual Film. London,
                       Oxford University Press, 1947.
                   Discusses the use, recommendations, and
                   policies for the non-theatrical film in London.

1926-1950   Rotha, Paul. Documentary Film. London,
                       Faber & Faber, 1963.
                   Considers the "documentary as the use of the
                   film medium to interpret creatively and in
                   social terms the life of the people as it exists
                   in reality." Includes index of film titles dis-
                   cussed and a list of 100 important documentary
                   films with credits.

1930-1945   Grierson, John. Grierson on Documentary,
                       comp. by Forsythe Hardy, with American
                       notes by Richard Griffith and Mary Losey.
                       N.Y., Harcourt, Brace, 1947.
                   A selection from the vast volume of film writing
                   and criticism Grierson produced between 1930
                   and 1945.

1930-1973   Impact Films, N.Y. Impact Films Catalog,
                       1974.
                   Catalog of documentary, experimental and fea-

ture films of the world's socially and political-
ly conscious works of cinema; contains lengthy
descriptions of the films; illustrated with stills.
Address: 144 Bleeker St.
New York, N.Y.   10012

1930-1975

Rehrauer, George.   The Short Film: an
Evaluative Selection of 500 Films.   N.Y.,
Macmillan, 1975.
A sourcebook of criticism of 16mm films in
all subject areas from the 1930s to the present
day; evaluations are by experts in many fields;
films are arranged alphabetically by title and
include release date, credits, running time,
type of film, description and suggested audience; stills included.

1933-1974

Illinois.   University, Champaign.   Educational
Films, 1972-75.
16mm rental catalog with a subject arrangement of documentary and factual films, international in coverage; gives synopsis and basic
information on each film.

1940-1948

Neergaard, Ebbe.   Documentary in Denmark.
Copenhagen, Statens Filmcentral, 1948.
One hundred films of fact in war, occupation,
liberation, peace, 1940-1948; a catalog with
synopsis.

1943-1971

McGraw-Hill Films, N.Y.   Selected Releases
from Contemporary Films, 1972-73.
Catalog of 16mm educational and documentary
films for rental or sale arranged by subject;
gives synopsis and descriptive material.

ca. 1950-1970

Rice, Susan.   Films Kids Like; a Catalog of
Short Films for Children.   Chicago, Center
for Understanding Media, 1973.
Gives synopsis, description, and other information on short documentary, factual films, international in coverage, including animated films;
illustrated with stills.   No film production dates
are given.

1952-1970

Rosenthal, Alan.   The New Documentary in
Action; a Casebook in Film Making.
Berkeley, University of California Press,
1971.
A collection of 17 film critiques and interviews
with leading directors from all film genres.

ca. 1960-1974

Time Life Films, N.Y.   Time Life Films Cata-

log, 1973-74.
A collection of nearly 700 16mm nontheatrical
films for rental or sale, mostly productions of
the British Broadcasting Corporation. A subject arrangement giving synopses, excerpts of
reviews, producer, illustrations; no dates of
production are given.

1970-   Film Review Index. Pasadena, California.
                    Audio-Visual Associates, Vol. 1, 1970-
               A serial published quarterly and international
               in coverage; an exhaustive index to critical re-
               views and evaluations of 16mm educational and
               informational motion pictures.

1970-   Multi Media Reviews Index. Ann Arbor,
                    Pierian Press, 1970-
               Annual index to reviews of media appearing in
               a great variety of periodicals and services.

1972-   Film Sneaks Annual. Ann Arbor, Pierian
                    Press, 1972-
               A guide to 4,500 non-theatrical films with
               ratings by librarians from 40 major libraries.

1972-   Kurtz, Alice S. and Kevin J. Kelly. The En-
                    vironment Film Review. N.Y., Environ-
                    ment Information Center, 1972-
               Under 21 major environmental categories, such
               as air pollution, wild life, etc., films are ar-
               ranged alphabetically; reviews give critical
               rating, length, purchase/rental, credits; pub-
               lished annually.

SPECIAL EFFECTS AND ANIMATED FILMS

1902-1956

Steinbrunner, Chris, and Burt Goldblatt. Cinema of the Fantastic. N.Y., Saturday Review Press, 1972.
Contains 15 extended film reviews, creating a developmental history of the fantasy film from "A Trip to the Moon" (1902) to "Forbidden Planet" (1956).

1902-1974

Brosnan, John. Movie Magic: The Story of the Special Effects in the Cinema. N.Y., St. Martin's Press, 1974.
Details the full story and accomplishments of special effects in films and the men who create them; coverage is from the beginning of motion pictures with "behind-the-camera" stories of all major films using special effects since 1902.

1907-1970

Holman, L. Bruce. Puppet Animation in the Cinema. Cranbury, N.J., A. S. Barnes, 1975.
Attempts to record the history and development of the art; includes a chronological filmography representative of the work of the world's puppet filmmakers, 1907-1970.

1913-1933

Eisner, Lotte H. The Haunted Screen; Expressionism in the German Cinema and the Influence of Max Reinhardt. Berkeley, University of California Press, 1969.
A survey of the intellectual, artistic and technical development of the German cinema during the last decade of the silent film period including a brief discussion of the sound period, 1913-1933.

1913-1971

United Films, Tulsa, Okla. 50 Years of Devils, Demons and Monsters. 1972.
Best examples of terror, mystery and suspense films, 1913-1971; gives lengthy descriptions, credits, stills; rental information.

1920-1973   Lee, Walt and Bill Warren, eds. <u>Reference</u>
                         <u>Guide to Fantastic Films</u>. Los Angeles,
                         Chelsea-Lee Books, 1972-1974. 3 vols.
                     Covers the full range of science fiction, fan-
                     tasy and horror films, 1920-1973; gives credits,
                     title variants, studios/distributors, film de-
                     scriptions, subject classification.

1922-1971   Finch, Christopher. <u>The Art of Walt Disney;</u>
                         <u>from Mickey Mouse to the Magic Kingdoms</u>.
                         N.Y., H. N. Abrams, 1973.
                     A full survey of the work of Walt Disney; takes
                     a serious look at his major achievements, pre-
                     senting them within the general context of his
                     work as a whole; covers Disney Productions
                     from 1922 through 1971; includes outstanding
                     illustrations.

1932-1974   Harryhausen, Ray. <u>Film Fantasy Scrapbook</u>.
                         2nd ed., Cranbury, N.J., A. S. Barnes,
                         1974.
                     Details 22 film fantasy masterpieces of special
                     effects from "King Kong" (1932) to "The Golden
                     Voyage of Sinbad" (1974).

1942-1972   Sitney, P. Adams. <u>Visionary Film: the</u>
                         <u>American Avant-Garde</u>. N.Y., Oxford
                         University Press, 1974.
                     An analysis of selected American films made
                     by independent film-makers. It attempts to
                     "isolate and describe the visionary strain within
                     the complex manifold of the American avant-
                     garde film." Covers a 30-year period from
                     "Meshes of the Afternoon" (1942) to "What's
                     Wrong with This Picture?" (1972).

LEADING REFERENCE GUIDES

Bessy, Maurice et Jean-Louis Chardans. Dictionnaire du Cinéma
    et de la Télévision. Paris, Jean-Jacques Pauvert, 1965-1971.
    4 vols.
Encyclopedia of biographical sketches, technical terms, bibliography,
subject areas, and various aspects of cinematography techniques.
International in scope; text in French. Illustrated with stills, drawings and historical photographs.

Cinéma d'Aujourd'hui. Paris, Seghers; N.Y., Crown.
A series of important film studies on various actors and directors;
covers career evaluation; stills, text in French. Some in the series
have been published in English.

The Films of.... Secaucus, N.J., Citadel Press.
A continuing series of pictorial volumes of the work of individual
stars, of period genres as in The Films of World War II, of subject groupings as in Pictorial History of Sex in Films. Each gives
complete filmography, biographical material, casts, credits, synopses, and excerpts from reviews; covers all periods.

Geduld, Harry M. and Ronald Gottesman. An Illustrated Glossary of
    Film Terms. N.Y., Holt, Rinehart and Winston, 1973.
A non-technical glossary of terms with pictorial illustrations con-
sisting of photographs and drawings and verbal illustrations to pertinent examples from a wide range of well-known films.

Gottesman, Ronald and Harry M. Geduld. Guidebook to Film.
    N.Y., Holt, Rinehart & Winston, 1972.
"An eleven-in-one reference" book answers a multitude of questions
which are not answered well, or not at all anywhere else. Sections
include: books and periodicals, reference works, screenplays,
series, theory, criticism and reviews, theses and dissertations
about films, museums and archives, film schools, distributors,
sources for stills, festivals, awards, terminology.

Griffith, Richard. The Movie Stars. N.Y., Doubleday, 1970.
A massive collection of pictures and comment; a detailed study
of the qualities, the makers and the personalities of the stars.

Griffith, Richard, and Arthur Mayer. The Movies. Rev. ed.
    N.Y., Simon & Schuster, 1970.
A history of motion pictures from the silents through the 60s;

considerable scholarship and rare stills pervail.

Halliwell, Leslie. The Filmgoer's Companion. 3rd ed. N.Y.,
    Hill and Wang, 1970.
Entries in one vast index include actors, directors, producers,
musicians, writers and photographers selected from the whole history of the cinema, with emphasis on Britain and Hollywood. Index
includes titles of films, series, subjects; gives birth and death
dates; credits.

The International Encyclopedia of Film, ed. by Roger Manvell.
    N.Y., Crown, 1972.
In alphabetic form, contains over 1,000 entries of biographies, national film histories, general topics, and technical terms; contains
some thousand stills, many in full color; chronological outline of
film history, bibliography, name index and film title index. Covers
75 years of the film.

International Film Guide Series, ed. by Peter Cowie. London, A.
    Zwemmer; N.Y., A. S. Barnes.
A continuing series of books about individual directors, actors and
types or periods in film. It includes "The Cinema of ..." series.
Each study includes a survey of the person or period giving criticism,
credits, stills.

Kaminsky, Stuart M. American Film Genres: Approaches to a
    Critical Theory of Popular Film. Dayton, Ohio, Pflaum/
    Standard, 1974.
A more serious analysis of the popular entertainment film in rela-
tion to better understanding other American cultural trends. Subjects covered are overview, the individual film, comparative forms,
literary adaptation and change, contemporary problems, variations
on a major genre, psychological considerations, performing arts,
history and social change.

Madsen, Roy Paul. The Impact of Film; How Ideas Are Communi-
    cated through Cinema and Television. N.Y., Macmillan, 1973.
Attempts to define how film and television programs are organized
for idea communication; provides a source work in four major divi-
sions: Concepts of Cinema-Television; The Dramatic Film; Documentary and Persuasive Forms; Educational and Research Forms.

Michael, Paul. The American Movies Reference Book: the Sound
    Era. Englewood Cliffs, N.J., 1969.
Divided into six sections: History, by decade from the '30s through
the '60s for films made during each 10-year period; Players, 600
are listed alphabetically, giving casts, credits; Directors, 50, with
credits; Producers, 50, with credits; Awards; Stills.

Minus, Johnny and William Storm Hale. Film Superlist: 20,000
    Motion Pictures in the Public Domain. Hollywood, Calif., 7
    Arts Press, 1973.
This massive reference book lists over 50,000 films, provides

copyright renewal information for over 25,000 films, and indicates over 20,000 films in the public domain.

Sadoul, Georges. Dictionary of Film Makers. Berkeley, University
    of California Press, 1972.
Gives biographical and career information on 1,000 directors, script-writers, cinematographers, art directors, composers, producers, inventors in the motion picture industry of the world.

Shipman, David. The Great Movie Stars: The Golden Years. N.Y.,
    Crown, 1970.
Biographical summary of some 160 stars, giving photos, critical quotes, opinions and statistical data from the silent era through 1945.

Shipman, David. The Great Movie Stars: The International Years.
    N.Y., St. Martin's Press, 1972.
A continuation of the above book, covers film performers 1945 to date; contains more than 220 capsule biographies; offering factual information and film criticism; stills.

La Storia del Cinema. Milan, Vallardi, 1966-67. 4 vols.
An encyclopedia of world cinema, with text in Italian; outstanding color stills with good coverage of films, players, and directors.

Vocabulaire du Cinéma. The Hague, Netherlands Government In-
    formation Service and Council for Cultural Co-operation of the
    Council of Europe, 1973.
A vocabulary of some 900 cinema terms in common use; text is given in French, English, Dutch, Italian, German, Spanish, and Danish.

The World Encyclopedia of the Film, ed. by Tim Cawkwell. N.Y.,
    World Publishing, 1972.
Reported to be the most comprehensive film encyclopedia in any language, containing breadth of selection with careful, detailed research and an unparalled degree of completeness within individual entries. Divided into two massive sections: biographies, and an index of film titles with main credits as mentioned in the book. Contains small identifying illustrations of scenes.

REPRESENTATIVE FILM DISTRIBUTORS' CATALOGS

Feature Films on 8mm and 16mm. 4th ed, comp. & ed. by James
L. Limbacher. N.Y., R. R. Bowker, 1974.
This book serves as an index to various distributors' catalogs, advising where to rent, purchase or lease more than 15,000 films.
Gives basic information about each film, addresses of film companies and distributors, distribution by area, and an index to directors.

The following is a list of some of the major film distributors
of films for rent and sale.

Blackhawk Films, The Eastin-Phelan Corp., Davenport, Iowa
52808. Bulletin.
Offering the "world's largest selection of things to show," twelve
bulletins are distributed during the year. In each issue a different
portion of the films have descriptions, so by keeping the bulletins
for three to four months, all descriptions for Blackhawk Films releases may be maintained. Offers films, slides and equipment for
sale.

Budget Films, Los Angeles. Catalog, 1973, 1974.
Catalog of rental films from "The Conjuror" (1899) to "I Never
Sang for My Father" (1971). Gives cast, synopsis; groupings by
type, documentaries, silent, musicals, foreign films, fantasy,
sports, westerns, short subjects, etc. Includes list of films by
directors as well as alphabetical index.
Address: 4590 Santa Monica Blvd.
Los Angeles, Calif. 90029

California. University. Extension Media Center. Films, 1975-
1976.
Contains concise, accurate information about the films in their collection; one of the most up-to-date collections, issued every two
years. Contains feature films in addition to educational and documentary films, giving synopses, rental or purchase information.
The first cumulation was 1965/69.
Address: University of California
Extension Media Center
Berkeley, Calif. 94720

Cinema Eight, Middlesex Ave., Chester, Conn. 06412. Catalog.
Offers for sale a large collection of 8mm and 16mm films.

Cinema 5, 595 Madison Ave., New York, N.Y. 10022.
Offers for rent a select collection of recent foreign and specialized
films.

Contemporary Films/McGraw-Hill, N.Y. Feature Film Collection.
16mm films for rental, dating back to 1919; films are grouped by
country of origin; gives synopses, excerpts from reviews; credits
and general information; stills. Other sectional catalogs are issued,
as English and Humanities, Science and Mathematics, and Solidgold,
a collection of short films.
Address: 330 West 42nd St.
          New York, N.Y. 10036

Em Gee Film Library, 4931 Gloria Ave., Encino, Calif. 91316.
   Catalog.
Sales and rentals of 16mm films; silent and early sound films from
various countries; extensive collection.

Essex Film Club, 263 Harrison St., Nutley, New Jersey 07110
Long established distributor of 8mm and 16mm classic films for
sale.

Films Incorporated, Wilmette, Ill. The Showcase Collection, 1973.
A rental collection of choice popular films from "Wings" (1928) to
1972. Basically the catalog is a collection of fine film posters in
color, with a visual index of films alphabetically by title, giving
stills, credits, synopses, and excerpts from reviews.
Address: 1144 Wilmette Ave.
          Wilmette, Ill. 60091

Gaines "16" Films, 1507 Stagg St., Van Nuys, Calif. 91405
Dealer in used and new 16mm films; offers monthly listings including features, trailers, clips, shorts, and television shows.

Grove Press Film Division, 53 East 11th St., New York, N.Y.
        10003. Film Catalog.
Offers a collection of short films, underground films, and international features for rental and sale.

Ivy Films, 165 West 46th St., New York, N.Y., 10036. Ivy Film/
   16.
Offers a large library of films for rental including many important
titles not previously available; catalog lists titles, stars, directors
and dates. Publishes catalogs of features, shorts, and serials.

Janus Films, N.Y. Janus Film Collection, 1974.
Film rental catalogs international in scope. The several catalogs
from this company are excellent for plots, casts, critical com-
ments, stills, posters, and film evaluation articles. Supplements
include: "The German Collection," "The French Collection," "The
Bergman Supplement," "The British Collection," and "Special Event
Cinema."
Address: 745 Fifth Avenue
          New York, N.Y. 10022

Kit Parker Films, Carmel Valley, Calif.   93924.   Catalog, 1975.
An independent 16mm film rental library of films.   The catalog is
descriptive and illustrated, offering American and foreign films from
silents to modern films.

Macmillan Audio Brandon Films.   16mm Collection of International
    Cinema, 1974-75.   Mount Vernon, N.Y.
Gives synopses, casts, credits, and critical comments on 1,000
feature films and 800 shorts.   Included are films of the silent era,
foreign and Hollywood classics, experimental and independent films.
International in scope.   Fully illustrated with stills.
Address: 34 MacQuesten Parkway So.
                Mount Vernon, N.Y.   10550

New Line Cinema, 121 University Place, New York, N.Y.   10003.
    Catalog.
Offers for rent classics, contemporary foreign, American independent,
experimental and porno films, most of which have never had an extensive theatrical release.

Pyramid Films, Santa Monica, Calif.   Pyramid Films, 71/72.
Short films, documentary, art films, experimental films dating
from 1897 to 1970.   Gives synopses, reviews, credits, stills.
Address: Box 1048
                Santa Monica, Calif.   90406

RBC Films, 933 North La Brea Ave., Los Angeles, Calif.   90038
Exclusive non-theatrical distributor for Chaplin feature films, and
recent big box-office releases made by BBS Productions.

Radim Films, N.Y.   Film Images, 1972.   2 vols.
Vol. 1 contains 16mm films on the arts, humanities, social sciences, natural sciences, and children's films.   Vol. 2 contains
16mm English and foreign language features from 1902-1970.
Synopsis, excerpts from reviews, credits, rental or sale information, stills are given.
Address: 17 West 60th St.
                New York, N.Y.   10023

Roa Films, Milwaukee, Wisconsin.   Film Rental Catalog, 1975-
    1976.
Alphabetical and subject arrangement of 16mm films for rental;
gives brief synopsis and credits; covers features, cartoons, silents,
shorts, educational, as values-discussion, drugs-safety, etc.
Address: 1696 North Astor St.
                Milwaukee, Wisconsin   53202

Swank Motion Pictures, Hollywood, Movies from Swank, 1974-75.
Catalog of 16mm movies for colleges and universities.   Gives
credits, synopses, quotes from reviews, stills, a great many in
color.   Includes classics as well as current films.
Address: 7073 Vineland Avenue
                North Hollywood, Calif.   91605

Time Life Films, N.Y.   Time Life Films Catalog, 1973-74.
A collection of 16mm nontheatrical films, mostly productions of
the British Broadcasting Corporation.   A subject arrangement giving
synopses, excerpts of reviews, producer, etc.
Address: 43 West 16th St.
           New York, N.Y.   10011

Trans-World Films, 332 South Michigan Ave., Chicago, Ill.   60604.
     Catalog.
Offers a select list of features for rent from France, Britain,
Spain, India, Japan, Belgium, Germany and the U.S.; also offers
a large range of animated shorts.

Twyman Films, Dayton, Ohio.   Twyman 1974 College Catalog.
Large collection of classic films, from the early silents to date.
Includes short films, cartoons.   Each film has synopsis, review
excerpts, credits, stills, awards and audience rating codes and
symbols.
Address: 329 Salen Avenue
           Dayton, Ohio   45401

United Films, Tulsa, Okla.   Catalog, 1974-75.
Catalog of classic and modern films, gives brief credits and synop-
ses, and basic information.
Address: 1425 South Main
           Tulsa, Oklahoma   74119

SOURCES FOR STILLS

The following is a list of dealers who can supply stills, posters, pressbooks, and other cinema memorabilia. In writing to these sources, it is advised that one enclose a self-addressed, stamped envelope.

Bond Street Book Store
    1638 N. Wilcox Ave.
    Hollywood, Calif.   90028
Mountains of stills and posters are available for sale at reasonable prices, but you have to go there and dig them out for yourself. Stills are from films approximately 1950 to date.   Some unusual "finds" may be unearthed if one has the time and patience to search.

Bruce Webster
    426 N.W. 20th St.
    Oklahoma City, Okla.   73103
Offers posters and other movie material, with a specialty in glass projection slides from old movies; publishes lists.

Burco Enterprises
    1370 Washington Ave.
    Miami Beach, Fla.   33139
Large collection of stills and candid photographs; carries from 30 to 50 different stills on each film as it is released.

Cecil J. Miller
    19 Washington St.
    P.O. Box G
    Calais, Me.   04619
Sells, buys or trades thousands of stills, with the emphasis on silents, serials, and westerns.

Cherokee Book Shop
    P.O. Box 3427
    6607 Hollywood Blvd.
    Hollywood, Calif.   90028
Offers unlimited sources of stills from the silents to Cinemascope.

Cine Books
    692a Young St.
    Toronto 5, Ontario, Canada

Canadian center for film books, posters, magazines; publishes catalog.

Cinefantastique
    P.O. Box 270
    Oak Park, Ill.   60303
Huge collection of stills, pressbooks, posters of all genres, but
specializes in science fiction, horror, and fantasy films.   CFQ
Stillshop provides a choice still selection of classic films; also
can provide film clips.

The Cinema Attic
    P.O. Box 7772
    Philadelphia, Pa.   19101
Can supply stills of thousands of film titles; search service; publishes catalog.

Cinema Book Shop
    13-14 Great Russell St.
    London, W.C. 1, England
Reputed to be one of the "world's most famous" sources of film
books, posters, press books, stills, and memorabilia.

Cinemabilia
    10 West 13th St.
    New York, N.Y.   10011
Reputed to be the "world's largest film bookshop and gallery," it
offers a huge display of pressbooks, sheet music, lobby cards,
posters, stills, books.   Publishes 270-page catalog.

Collectors Book Store
    6763 Hollywood Blvd.
    Hollywood, Calif.   90028
Reputed to have 1,000,000 stills available from 1916 to date; also
specializes in movie and TV scripts.

Collectors Corner
    P.O. Box 8021
    Universal City, Calif.   91608
Offers posters, stills, magazines, sound track show recordings for
sale, trade, or will purchase.

Eddie Brandt's Saturday Matinee
    P.O. Box 3232
    6501 Lankershim Blvd.
    North Hollywood, Calif.   91609
Reputed to be "the world's second largest collection" of movie stills,
posters, lobby cards, pressbooks, autographs, programs, etc.

Gary Levinson
    500 N.E. 161st St.
    North Miami Beach, Fla.   33162
Stills, pressbooks, posters, etc. with emphasis on science fiction,
horror, and fantasy films.

George Theofiles
    Miscellaneous Man Antiques
    1728 Thames St.
    Baltimore, Md.   21231
Poster specialists; buys and sells American posters printed before
1945 and European posters printed before 1925.

Hampton Books
    Rt. 1, Box 76
    Newberry, S.C.   29108
Old-established mail order firm publishes regular catalog, Cinema 6,
which lists over 1,000 items on cinema and television history and
theory: offers books, magazines, stills, posters, and other memorabilia.

Hollywood Poster Exchange
    7250 Beverly Blvd.
    Room 102
    Los Angeles, Calif.   90036
Outstanding selection of stills, posters, lobby cards, 1936 to date;
buy, sell, or trade.

The Hollywood Review: Movie Memorabilia
    1523 North La Brea Ave.
    Hollywood, Calif.   90028
Offers huge selection of photographs plus a research service in
locating particular stills.   Uses a unique feature of providing Xerox
copies of stills to the researcher in order to avoid duplication of
purchases.   Stills are custom printed.   Formerly known as Quality
First.

John E. Allen's Friendly Service
    92 Highland St.
    Park Ridge, N.J.   07656
Stills, posters, books, magazines and films bought and sold.

Keir's Celebrity Photos
    1143 Sixth Ave.
    New York, N.Y.   10003
Long established shop at 6th & 44th Sts., offers a good selection
of stills.   No lists issued.

Kenneth G. Lawrence
    Movie Memorabilia Shop of Hollywood
    P.O. Box 29027
    Los Angeles, Calif.   90029
Reputed to have the "world's largest stock of movie stills, posters,
pressbooks, production scenes, candids, portraits." Publishes a
catalog of 15,000 films and 5,000 players.

Larry Edmunds Book Shop
    6658 Hollywood Blvd.
    Hollywood, Calif.   90028

Reputed to be "the world's largest collection" of books and related
material dealing with motion pictures, biographies, posters, lobby
cards, pressbooks, autographs, and stills. Publishes the 524-page
Cinema Catalog.

Mark Frank
    801 Ave. C
    Brooklyn, N.Y. 11218
Buys, sells, or trades stills, pressbooks, photoplays, and 16mm
films.

Morris Everett, Jr.
    1460 Union Commerce Bldg.
    Cleveland, Ohio 44115
Buys, sells, or exchanges stills, souvenir books, pressbooks, posters, 1927 to date.

Movie Star News
    212 East 14th St.
    New York, N.Y. 10003
Long-established dealer in movie stills offering a huge collection;
publishes regular illustrated bulletin listing stills arranged by type,
genre; gives number of stills available on each title; search service.

Normand François Lareau
    Stills from Foreign Films
    227 East 81st St.
    New York, N.Y. 10028
Publishes lists of stills available from foreign films; stills are
selected primarily for content and design.

Nostalgia
    3220 Stanford
    Dallas, Texas 75225
Supplies stills, records, magazines, biographies; search service;
purchases all types film.

Orlo Bainbridge, Jr.
    Memory House
    P.O. Box 17416
    Tampa, Fla. 33612
Sells or trades copies only of original stills, 1915 to date; dis-
tributes lists.

Phibes Bros.
    P.O. Box 8536
    Baltimore, Md. 21234
Has thousands of stills and pressbooks issued during the 60s and
70s; send want list.

Photo Archives
    Room 709
    1472 Broadway
    New York, N.Y. 10036

Offers theatre and film collection of rare programs, sound tracks, theatre LPs, stills, personality files. No phone or mail orders.

Robert E. Scherl
    P.O. Box 2712
    Hollywood, Calif. 90028
Offers to sell or trade large collection of stills; emphasis is on the horror film.

Slides Over Hollywood
    7861 Oceanus Dr.
    Hollywood, Calif. 90046
Offers artistic selection of famous posters of films from the 30s and 40s on slides.

Stephen Sally
    Times Square Station
    P.O. Box 646
    New York, N.Y. 19936
Reputed to be "one of the largest collections of star photos and movie scenes in the world," covering 40 years of cinema. Publishes bulletins; Stephen Sally's Movie Goer, Star Portraits, and Scene Catalog, list items offered for stills, posters, pressbooks, portraits, and movie books.

INDEX